revenue
disruption

GAME-CHANGING
SALES AND MARKETING
STRATEGIES TO
ACCELERATE GROWTH

revenue
disruption

PHIL FERNANDEZ

WILEY

John Wiley & Sons, Inc.

For general information on our other products and services or for technical support, please contact our Customer Care Department within the United States at (800) 762-2974, outside the United States at (317) 572-3993 or fax (317) 572-4002.

Wiley publishes in a variety of print and electronic formats and by print-on-demand. Some material included with standard print versions of this book may not be included in e-books or in print-on-demand. If this book refers to media such as a CD or DVD that is not included in the version you purchased, you may download this material at http://booksupport.wiley.com. For more information about Wiley products, visit www.wiley.com.

ISBN: 978-1-118-29929-6 (cloth)
ISBN: 978-1-118-33189-7 (ebk)
ISBN: 978-1-118-33412-6 (ebk)
ISBN: 978-1-118-33524-6 (ebk)

Printed in the United States of America

10 9 8 7 6 5 4 3 2 1

CONTENTS

ACKNOWLEDGMENTS

Many of the ideas in this book are the result of years of discussion and collaboration among my colleagues at Marketo, as well as with a number of industry experts and thought leaders who have a shared interest in changing the way companies create revenue. And of course, I've learned more than anything from the innovative revenue leaders who are putting these ideas into action in their own companies. I'd like to thank the many colleagues, friends, and customers of Marketo who lent wisdom, case studies, and quotes to this effort.

I would like to extend special thanks to Jon Miller, my co-founder at Marketo. Jon is himself a prolific writer and thinker on the topic of modern demand marketing, and his assistance with the material in Part III was invaluable.

I'm not sure what I was thinking by embarking on this book project while at the same time doing my day job as CEO of a fast-growing software company. A successful result was only possible because of the amazing coordination and editorial assistance provided by Lori Bush Shepard, Sharon Seitz, and Peter Longini.

Thank you to Gaurav Kotak, who supported me by performing much of the original research cited in the book. Thank you also to the intrepid team at LaunchSquad, for helping me put Revenue Performance Management on the map.

I must also thank my husband, Daniel Sternbergh, for his encouragement, and for accepting with a smile all the nights, weekends, vacations, and holidays when I was spending time in front of a keyboard instead of with him.

This book would not have been possible without Patrick Di Chiro, a longtime marketing leader and consultant. Patrick and I spent many hours in wide-ranging and immensely enjoyable discussions that zigged and zagged from presidential politics to technology trends to wine, and of course, to Revenue Performance Management. It was through these discussions that the concept and outline for *Revenue Disruption* emerged, and Patrick's continuing mentoring and advice is reflected everywhere in the text.

Finally, I would like to thank Bruce Cleveland, a longtime Silicon Valley executive and venture capitalist. Bruce became the first venture investor in my company, Marketo, based on a vision that he and I share about the transformative power of Revenue Performance Management. Soon after investing in Marketo in late 2006, Bruce suggested that I write a book. The very concept frankly scared me, and for years, my ideas weren't well enough formed to undertake the effort. Over time, the topic of a book became a running joke between Bruce and me, often coming up in Marketo Board of Directors' meetings where I would use the phrase "The Book"—in quotes—to signify this unachieved project.

Bruce, it is a delight to present to you "The Book."

INTRODUCTION

In 1985, I was a young software engineering manager just a couple of years out of college, and was beginning to put down roots in the first home I could call my own. I still distinctly remember my trip to a local appliance store to buy my first clothes washer and dryer. These were still the days of the lonely "Maytag Repairman"—an advertising icon from my childhood that stood for reliability.

But which brand of appliance should I actually *buy*, I wondered. It felt like a big decision and there were lots of competing choices. I wanted to pick the highest quality model I could find, but my expectations were low. That's because I knew that washers or dryers broke down frequently, and that it wouldn't be long—maybe a year or two—before I could expect to spend a day home from work, waiting for the repairman to show up. Eventually, of course, the repairman did come—actually a number of times over the years that those first appliances lasted.

I found myself once again in the market for a washer and dryer last year, and this time I wanted the best of a new generation of ultra-low-water, low-energy appliances. So after a quick price check online, I was once again off to my local appliance store. But as I was looking at the different brands lined up in front of me, I had a sudden realization: My expectations had changed completely from my previous time around. Now, I expected that the washer and dryer would last forever, or at least until my retirement, and that I would be both shocked and disappointed if I ever needed service during that time.

The difference in my outlook was due to a quarter century of continuous manufacturing improvement, often referred to as Six Sigma. Companies had begun to adopt Six Sigma processes around the time I bought that first washer and dryer, and it produced huge improvements in quality, such as reduced defects, lowered costs, and infrequent repairs. This process had fundamentally reinvented society's expectations about product and service quality.

Around the same time I bought that first washer and dryer, I also ordered an amazing new personal computer for my home—an IBM PC/XT. I remember ordering the new toy, and waiting, and waiting, wondering when it would be delivered. I was told it would take about six weeks, but no one really knew for sure.

Fast-forward to spring 2011, when I ordered a new Apple iPad 2. From the instant I placed the order, I could track my newest new toy from its manufacture and engraving in Shenzhen, China, then on to Hong Kong, to Anchorage, and then to my front doorstep in California. And the whole process took less than a week.

As with Six Sigma, the emergence of the global real-time supply chain has transformed the world in which we live. Not only can we track our goods around the world with a touch on a screen, but the entire operation of the global economy has changed completely. Not very long ago, large companies had trillions of dollars tied up in inventory, whereas today, brands like Apple maintain less than five days of inventory in their supply chain.

Let's roll the clock back one more time. I remember when I became a manager at a hot Silicon Valley start-up in the mid-1980s that my phone would ring three or four times a day with a salesperson trying to pitch me some new product or service. Back then, I still answered the phone when it rang, and I'd find myself saying over and over, "No, I'm not interested," and trying to hang up quickly without being too rude.

Last week, I counted more than 25 voice mail messages on my office phone, each of them from a salesperson trying to pitch his or her latest wares. I just don't answer my phone nowadays—and neither do most people I know. We simply can't. Ninety-nine out of a hundred are just another unwanted sales attempt, an expensive, unproductive, cold call that's frustrating to both me and to the poor salesperson doing the calling.

Despite all of the business changes we've seen over the past quarter century—Six Sigma's radically improved manufacturing productivity and quality; real-time supply chain management's drastically reduced inventories and lowered costs; the emergence of the World Wide Web; ubiquitous mobile computing; virtual tele-presence meetings; social media networks, and so forth—there is one facet of modern business that remains stubbornly stuck in the mud, and it is this:

The core processes that many global companies use to generate revenue—finding prospective buyers and selling to them—have changed little, if at all, over our lifetimes. The cold call is still king. Salespeople still attend training classes with a fundamental curriculum that hasn't changed in 50 years. Marketing professionals continue to be stereotyped as expensive artistes, preoccupied with picking colors and issuing press releases.

As a result, creating revenue—arguably the most important thing *any* business does—remains one of its most expensive and inefficient processes. Depending on the industry and its maturity, an organization will likely spend 20 or 30 percent or more of their total revenue on marketing and sales to create *more* revenue. This means that even a small improvement in the productivity and effectiveness of these processes can boost the competitiveness, growth, and profitability of a business.

The opportunity is enormous. That's because many otherwise-modern businesses use methods to create revenue that are at best obsolete, and at worst, totally dysfunctional. The entire revenue creation process is ripe for disruption, reimagination, and fundamental reinvention. In the pages ahead, I will outline a whole new set of management concepts about the organizations, business processes, software systems, and metrics used for revenue generation. I will describe a breakthrough approach called Revenue Performance Management, or RPM, that shatters archaic approaches to marketing and sales while providing the blueprint for building a far more effective and efficient revenue process in both large and small companies.

There are many strategic business initiatives that offer great opportunity. We've seen it before with Six Sigma and real time supply chain initiatives. But in the end, most are optional. Executive management can decide—perhaps at their peril, but still at their discretion—whether to embrace a bold new strategy or sit on the sidelines. Revenue Performance Management is different. This book argues that adopting an RPM strategy is not optional; it's essential. Every corporation can either embrace these ideas, or run the serious risk of falling into the dustbin of dysfunction and obsolescence.

Why? Simply put, it's because your buyers have already made the decision for you. The last two decades have seen the emergence of the World Wide Web, the explosive growth of Google, the ubiquitous presence of Amazon.com and other e-commerce sites, along with a profound shift in our culture revolving around digital media. And the pace of change has radically accelerated more recently with the astonishing growth of social media sites like Facebook, LinkedIn, and Twitter, as well as the increasingly ubiquitous experience of being connected on smart mobile devices 24/7. These changes have completely, totally, and permanently changed our expectations, both as consumers and buyers.

Yet marketing and sales processes have not kept pace with these changes, particularly in the realm of business-to-business revenue models, but also in many parts of the consumer world. The revenue creation process needs its own Six Sigma, and its own version of a real-time supply chain. All companies need to implement a completely new marketing and sales paradigm that embraces the global technological, cultural, and media changes that have forever transformed the buying and selling process.

Given the urgency of these issues, you can think of this book as a manifesto for change. Part I begins by taking stock of where most businesses are in their revenue creation process today, and how they got there. I elaborate on this notion that buying, and therefore selling and marketing, have fundamentally changed, and I make the case that adoption of RPM is not optional.

Part II examines the path toward transforming the revenue model. In particular, it explores ways in which the marketing team must take the lead in guiding this transformation. Part III takes a close look at the specific business tactics and processes that must be adopted, changed, or radically reinvented to survive in our changed revenue world.

And finally, we see the payoff in the concluding Part IV of the book, where we combine these concepts to formulate an action plan that will guide your company's adoption of Revenue Performance Management and its reinvention of both the marketing and sales functions. It's an ambitious goal. But companies worldwide are already doing this, and those who complete that journey can increase their revenue-generating capacities by 40 percent or more.

Most people say they want change, and they probably do, except when it affects them personally. Change can be difficult and scary. But avoiding it isn't always an option. After all, the change in buying patterns we're discussing here has already taken place. Businesses must therefore respond to that change and seize the opportunity that this new world of revenue creation has generated.

Decades ago, a revolution in manufacturing methods began to render home appliance breakdowns less frequent. It disrupted the repair industry, and made the Maytag Repairman feel so lonely. Today, we're in the middle of an equally disruptive revolution in managing revenue performance. But you don't need to feel lonely or left out. I hope this manifesto will help unleash your passion for revenue performance improvement as you put the techniques you'll learn here to use in your company.

PART I

THE PROBLEM

Causes and Consequences of Revenue Dysfunction

CHAPTER 1

It's the Buyer, Stupid

In 1992, political consultant James Carville cleared the path to Bill Clinton's election as President with one simple phrase: "It's the economy, stupid." There were plenty of other issues upon which Clinton could have built a campaign at that time. But his singular focus on the economy gave his campaign such clarity that it not only won him the election; it entered popular culture as an enduring meme.

The fundamental idea behind reinventing revenue is just as clear and simple: "It's the buyer, stupid." Revenue-generating organizations can worry all they want about tactics like trade show booths, targeted e-mail blasts, the number of cold calls made each day, expert negotiating skills, and whether SPIN Selling or Target Account Selling is really the best way to the money. But none of that really matters in the end. By the time that your prospective buyers see your trade show booth, read your e-mail, answer the phone, or tell you about their budget, they have already made up their minds.

In fact, your target buyers started making up their minds before you even knew they existed. This occurred when they visited your website and poked around in almost complete anonymity. Did they like what they found? Did they encounter current, relevant, and helpful information that educated them about why they should buy from you and not from your competitor? They probably asked their Facebook or LinkedIn friends and connections about whom to choose and whom to avoid. Did any advocates for your brand or product speak up? Do you even know who your advocates are? Sadly, most organizations today are likely to answer *no*.

Once a prospective buyer began to interact with your website, or your fan page, or clicked on one of your expensive Google AdWords, did you capture his or her attention and interest? Did you start to build a relationship? Maybe, or maybe not. All too often, a click on one online ad just leads to another irrelevant ad. Or a visit to a fan page leads to a fun experience, but not a relevant one for the buyer.

Sometimes, though, you get lucky; the prospect likes what you have to say and consents to give you his or her name, e-mail address, and maybe even a phone number. You have a lead. Quick! Get that lead in the hands of a salesperson. There's a live one on the line!

Oops! Not so fast. In a scene that's repeated over and over and over, the first call to that live one goes nowhere. It doesn't matter whether you're selling software, accounting services, a home equity loan, a wonderful new plastic polymer, or any other good or service. The story is the same: Your prospect doesn't even answer the phone. And if they do, they say something like, "No thanks. I was just doing some research."

This scenario is worse than simply being inefficient and frustrating for both the buyer and seller. It's also at the root of one of the most persistent dysfunctions of revenue organizations everywhere.

Here's how it usually goes: The marketing team hooks the live one on the web or through some other marketing program. It goes over the wall to sales, where the "no thanks" call happens. This scenario doesn't need to repeat itself too many times before sales decides that those live ones coming over the wall are really just old tires snagged on the end of the fishing line. So, no more frustrating, inefficient calls ever get made. Why bother, they figure. The leads from marketing are worthless.

The situation is just as hopeless on the other side of the wall. Marketing knows their website is current and compelling, that its AdWords were exactly targeted, and that the target buyer clicked (and yes, Google collected their fee for it). Yet nothing came of it because sales never made the call. That's demoralizing at best, and at worst, a recipe for a budget cut in marketing.

There is a common theme running through both sides of the story: In each case, the revenue professionals in marketing or sales acted as though *they* were in control of the situation, executing their carefully devised plan, making a cold call, sending an e-mail, or pouncing on the live one. Unfortunately, no one clued the buyer in to these grand plans. The buyer was simply conducting his or her own process, following his or her own plan and schedule. They'll talk to you if and when they want to, but not necessarily when *you* want to talk to them. The buyer is in control of the entire experience.

This is a new notion for many organizations. It wasn't very long ago that buyers were at the mercy of the salesperson for even the most basic information. There was almost no other way to learn about a product or service in enough detail to make a quality buying decision. However, the web and social media have changed all of this.

THE NEW SHOWROOM FLOOR

The way people buy cars today provides a vivid illustration of just how fast and completely the Internet has changed the buying process. Less than a generation ago, new car buyers had only a handful of independent information resources to help them make a decision about what make or model to purchase. Beyond automakers' mass advertising and reading reviews in popular car magazines, buyers were essentially forced to trek from one dealer showroom to another to get a feel for their choices and start to make a decision. And the dealer's sales staff remained firmly in charge of the interaction at each car lot, so much so that the image of a high-pressure car salesman has grown to almost iconic proportions in our popular culture.

Fast-forward to the current day, and all of this has been turned upside down. According to a 2007 Yahoo!-Polk study, fully 88 percent of all car shoppers started their process with online research before ever walking into a dealership. The web is now teeming with resources, such as the remarkable 3-D interactive buying tools hosted by most major auto brands. Competitive pricing information is readily available on the web; look it up on a web buyer's guide, or ask your Facebook friends what they paid.

As a result, most auto buyers never visit a dealer until they have already made up their mind about the specific made and model they intend to buy. In fact, one recent CarsOnline poll revealed that

44 percent of new car buyers would never visit a traditional auto dealer *at all* if given the option; they'd instead choose to complete the entire process online. The buyer is literally in the driver's seat, and in total control.

It's the buyer, stupid.

Ultimately, the transformative opportunity described in this book leads back to one simple idea: Power has shifted from seller to buyer in a profound and permanent way. Just as Bill Clinton's first presidential campaign relentlessly zeroed in on the economy, it is essential that companies take an equally sharp focus on their buyers instead of on their own tactics. Yet marketing and sales teams in countless organizations have failed to fully acknowledge this development; they continue to cling to the old ways and resist change. This is not sustainable, especially since change is already here. And the first step to embracing it is to understand what you're changing *from*. As such, the following chapters will explore where most organizations are today in the arts and crafts of marketing and sales.

KEY POINTS

- Keeping a laser-like focus on the buyer, instead of on a company's own internal politics and business processes, is essential for effective revenue performance.

- Prospective buyers typically do a lot of research into a company and its products before the company even knows they exist.

- The marketing department's traditional practice of handing off leads to sales is both mutually frustrating and unrealistic in today's marketplace.

- It is today's buyer—not the supplier's sales or marketing people—who controls the process leading toward a sale.

CHAPTER 2

The Selling Cry of the Lonely Hunter

Not long ago, I spoke with a customer who recounted an experience she had at a week-long class offered by one of the better-known sales training organizations. I'm sure you know the kinds of classes I am talking about. They're promoted with emphatic headlines, screaming things like, "GET THEM TO YES!" and "SELLING HUNGRY!" And that's just the advertising to get you to sign up. Once she took the class itself, she described almost cult-like scenes that seemed frozen in the past. Our customer was one of only three women who attended the seminar, and she didn't appreciate the seminar leader's characterization of his wife as the "best salesperson of all . . . because she got me to buy her so much jewelry."

But what really turned this customer off was not so much the class leader's use of cheesy anecdotes to rev up the attendees. It was the anachronistic and stubbornly old-school sales strategies that were elevated to the position of holy writ. She recounted two frequently used metaphors during the session that underscored her point. The first is the hoary old image of "every salesperson is a lonely hunter." In other words, each is out there on the Serengeti on his or her own, hunting for big game, and will only eat if they find something to kill.

The second theme of the class was that of the salesperson as "king." In it, the guy (since this class, like most, was oriented toward males) must do battle every day to bring the bounty (i.e., sales revenues) back to the hungry hordes at the waiting castle. While this Knights of the Round Table imagery holds a certain appeal to sales training companies, it is about as relevant to the current business environment as Sir Lancelot and his jousting exploits.

Their picturesque charm aside, the "lonely hunter" and "king" metaphors share a stereotypic and outmoded view of both the sales process and profession. Even more important, they vividly illustrate the obsolete character of the dominant marketing and sales model. This model has to change if corporations are ever to maximize their full revenue generating potential.

IT TAKES A VILLAGE

An effective salesperson in today's digitally networked, social media–driven world can no more stand alone as a solitary hunter than they can stand above everyone else as king of the revenue hill. Instead, it takes a whole revenue village—a fully connected, highly collaborative village populated by creative brand marketing specialists, demand marketing superstars, pile-driving sales development representatives, enlightened revenue leaders, and great team-oriented sales professionals—to be truly successful today.

Sales can no longer operate in the old battle-hardened silos we've all come to know. Under that scenario, the sales team would emerge from its silo only to take leads from marketing, and then probably drop those leads on the floor, after which it would go forth to do battle with prospects and vanquish the sale.

Far from operating as solo hunters, salespeople today must instead be hyper-connected. They need to link up with fellow sales professionals, as well as to their colleagues from marketing, research, customer support, and technology. Most importantly, they need access to the same information sources and online social networks that their prospects are almost certainly using.

The concept of salesperson as king is made even less relevant by the radical changes in the buyer/seller dynamic that we discussed in the previous chapter. Today's buyers have instant access via the web, search, and increasingly social media to valuable information, data, reviews, referrals, and friends' recommendations. Armed with this sort of timely and relevant information, the buyer now is indisputably the king of the sales deal, and can then dictate when and how he or she wants to interact with the "revenue village."

Revenue as a Process

The dated view of sales professionals as lone wolves and kings of their territories is actually a symptom of a much larger problem: the way in which far too many companies still view the revenue process. At the core, they don't see revenue as the product of a designed, measured, and optimized process. Rather, they consider that revenue is created through a series of disconnected steps, starting with the creation of awareness and leads by the marketing department and concluding with their sales staff closing the sale. In the worst-case scenario, they perceive revenue generation to be the heroic job of individual salespeople. To these individuals, the very concept that the marketing team could actually be part of the revenue equation is entirely foreign.

I will describe later in this book how revenue generation follows a clearly defined cycle—one that demands an integrated approach from marketing and sales teams working together collaboratively. That holistic revenue process is about as similar to the old model touted to this day in sales classes as an Apple iPad is to a vintage IBM Selectric typewriter.

Today's radically altered business and technology environment, where the buyer is truly king, presents real challenges to both marketing and sales professionals. But it also provides tremendous opportunities for corporations to commit to and implement an entirely new way of creating, managing, and accelerating their revenue. And none of it has anything to do with hunters or kings.

Key Points

- The use of metaphors that depict salespeople as lonely hunters or sovereign kings is misleading nowadays. Creating revenue is a collaborative enterprise between marketing and sales teams—not one that anyone can perform solely on his or her own.

- Today's salespeople need to be highly connected to their fellow sales professionals, as well as to their colleagues in marketing, research, customer support, and technology.

- Today's buyers are highly informed about possible purchases from multiple sources; the customer now drives the selling process.

CHAPTER 3

Before and After Mad Men
A Brief History of Marketing

Chapter 1 mentioned the process that marketing teams use to hook live ones—in other words, new leads—and throw them over the wall to sales. But just as the hunters and kings who populate traditional sales jobs need to reinvent their approach, the marketing function requires its own revolution. Although the role of marketing has evolved over the years, especially in the post-World War II modern era of marketing, it is surprising how much it has remained the same considering today's digital world. That, of course, is part of the dysfunction that this book describes. We need to disrupt, deconstruct, and fundamentally reinvent traditional marketing roles and responsibilities. But just who are the fishermen and women who cast their lines for live leads, and how did they come to be?

Marketing as we currently know it traces its roots to the Industrial Revolution of the eighteenth and nineteenth centuries, which were periods of rapid and massive social, technological, and scientific upheaval (sound familiar?). The job of marketing began to emerge as a distinct profession when the mass production of goods became separated from their consumption; in the old days, consumers really did "eat what they killed."

As industrialization expanded and breakthroughs in transportation opened up new markets, formerly lengthy supply chains shrank and competition increased. Customers began to realize for the first time that they could actually choose among competing goods and services. Companies introduced product branding, accompanied by rival claims and promises. So how was a customer supposed to make up his or her mind when faced with this new array of choices? That's when the new marketing professional stepped in, charged with the task—to put it gently—of "guiding" consumer choice.

"THEY LAUGHED WHEN I SAT DOWN . . ."

Throughout the first half of the twentieth century and beyond, those early marketers didn't have very many options for communicating information to buyers. They typically relied on clever messages that they hoped would influence attitudes and shape buying behavior. Marketing communication was entirely one way: The seller would talk, and the buyer would read, listen to, or watch print ads, radio spots, and later TV commercials.

Their limited ability to convey information meant that, while marketers could pass along a broad concept, an image, and a name, they didn't really have the opportunity to communicate or relate detailed information to individual customers. That was the salesperson's job; he or she could meet one-on-one with the buyer, engage in two-way conversation, and close the information gap between buyer and seller.

The dawn of the brand-marketing era saw early advertising agencies emerge and refine the process of brand creation in the consumer's mind. In hindsight, many of those early campaigns' naïveté and stereotypic views of consumers seem laughable. Eventually, though, advertising emerged as something close to a high art form, becoming a staple of modern culture.

FIGURE 3.1   John Caples was a fledgling copywriter in 1926 when he wrote what is widely considered to be one of the most famous advertising headlines of all time.

CORE MARKETING PHILOSOPHIES TAKE SHAPE

Around the middle of the 1950s, marketers began flexing their muscles and the modern day marketing department began to take shape. Many of the strategic, research, and media related methodologies developed during this mid-twentieth century that we now refer to as the *Mad Men* era (owing to the highly acclaimed cable TV show) are still used widely to this day. An intellectual foundation began to emerge that saw marketing as its own distinct profession. It was captured in a set of ideas that has come to be called the marketing concept philosophy, meant to differentiate marketing from an earlier concept built around a sales-focused model of buyer engagement.

It is the same philosophical framework that students on the marketing track in most business schools learn today. So it's worth understanding a bit about these philosophies and the grounding professional marketers bring to the job. This will help us identify which concepts are worth keeping and which ones need to go as we retool both marketing and sales to accelerate revenue growth.

Professor Richard L. Sandhusen, whose textbooks on marketing are used in business schools worldwide, identifies three distinct philosophies of marketing: as a business concept, as a societal concept, and as a concept of relationships. In essence:

1. The Marketing Concept Philosophy

    Defined as an integrated customer- and profit-oriented philosophy of business, the marketing concept philosophy differs from predecessor philosophies that emphasized products ("a good product will sell itself") and selling ("don't sell the steak, sell the sizzle") in a number of significant ways:

    a. The marketing concept defines the firm's mission in terms of benefits and satisfactions it offers customers, rather than the products it makes and sells.

    b. It emphasizes using two-way communication to identify customer needs and then develops and markets products and services to satisfy these needs. Gone is the stress on one-way communication to persuade people to buy products already made.

c. It highlights the fact that both long- and short-range
    planning are needed to achieve profit by meeting cus-
    tomer need. Gone is an exclusive focus on short-range
    planning to achieve sales volume objectives.

    In recent years, the marketing concept philoso-
    phy—that of working back from defined customer needs
    to marketing offerings that have been calculated to satisfy
    them—has come under attack. Some critics claim that
    this "customer knows best" approach panders to diverse
    needs and is wasteful in this era of shortages and environ-
    mental concerns.

2. The Societal Marketing Concept Philosophy

    This marketing philosophy, which responds to critics
    of the marketing concept philosophy, doesn't oppose the
    free-enterprise notion of determining and delivering target
    markets' needs more effectively than competitors. However,
    it does maintain that brands should deliver these satisfac-
    tions in a way that also enhances society's well-being. It
    claims that marketing managers should balance three inter-
    ests in setting policies and formulating marketing plans: the
    buyer, the seller, and society at large. A good example of
    this is bottle laws that mandate concern for the environment
    among soft drink companies.

3. The Relationship Philosophy

    A marketing philosophy evolved around the turn of
    the millennium that stressed long-term value-added rela-
    tionships with customers. Justifying this philosophy was the
    notion that it was a lot less expensive (and therefore more
    profitable) to maintain and increase business with exist-
    ing customers than to find new ones, and that customers
    themselves usually prefer this approach. Like the societal
    marketing philosophy, relationship marketing goes beyond
    customers to stress loyalty and strong working relations with
    suppliers, employees, and other stakeholders. It also empha-
    sizes teamwork and well trained, customer oriented person-
    nel with authority to make decisions and solve problems.

THE GOOD, THE BAD, AND THE UGLY

This is pretty high-concept stuff: "benefits and satisfactions of customers," "the well-being of society," and "long-term value-added relationships." What do we make of this?

The Good

It's hard to argue with any of these as philosophies, although one wonders how helpful they are to a front-line marketing professional under the gun to launch a new campaign. Even so, they contain some pretty solid practical ideas—specifically, the notions of "two-way communication to identify customer need," "long- and short-range planning to achieve profit," and "teamwork and well-trained, customer-oriented personnel." We'll keep each of these ideas in our blueprint for accelerating revenue growth.

The Bad

While the relationship marketing concept does in fact call for teamwork, I am struck by how insular these philosophies appear when read as a whole. They are about the marketing department setting policies and formulating plans basically on its own. Indeed, each of these marketing concepts evolved in response to earlier sales-oriented models of buyer engagement. Notice the complete lack of any hints as to how we might harmonize any marketing and sales philosophy.

The Ugly

While the guiding philosophies of marketing continue to evolve, neither the academic discipline of marketing nor the day-to-day operation of the marketing function itself have managed to keep pace with the massive changes in media, technology, and culture that have occurred. In particular, there is a striking absence from any of these philosophies any recognition of the fundamental power shift from the company and its marketing department to the buyer. Buyers define "benefits and satisfactions" for themselves in this new world, often on Twitter, Facebook, and LinkedIn. They aren't satisfied to just provide input on long-range product cycles. They want to ask questions, get answers on their timeline, and carry out their own self-directed research.

If you disregard the incessant smoking, the snappy suits, and the absence of women executives, *Mad Men*'s fictionalized view of marketing is remarkably close to what still happens in today's marketing departments. And that's especially puzzling in light of the fact that marketing people like to think of themselves as change agents living on the bleeding edge of emerging trends. It is a lapse that must be fixed.

KEY POINTS

- The discipline of marketing grew out of the Industrial Revolution and the separation of production from consumption.

- Early marketing communications provided a limited amount of generic information and imagery; salespeople provided more detailed and personalized versions.

- Marketing philosophy evolved over time from its focus on serving the company and its products to that of serving society and then to emphasizing the value of long-term relationships.

- The evolution of the marketing concept tended to uncouple marketing from sales.

CHAPTER 4

Demand Generation Emerges

As marketing organizations came into their own over the past half-century, specialties within the discipline began to emerge, triggered by the concurrent emergence of global brands, sophisticated academic frameworks, and new digital marketing technologies. Some marketing professionals gravitated toward the "softer" side of the profession—design, communications, brand—while others preferred to work on the product side and become experts in describing, positioning, and pricing.

Of course, the nature of buying—and therefore the marketing required to encourage buying—differs for various kinds of products and services. For a wide array of consumer goods, powerful brand identity and clever promotions like coupons and loyalty programs are proven ways to spur buying. Those branding campaigns have leapfrogged, essentially unchanged, directly into the newest social media channels.

For other kinds of buying, however, it's just not enough to create an image, an impression, an aspiration, or a discount deal, and hope that customers will buy. Customers who spend hundreds, thousands, or even millions on a purchase need to be a bit more deliberate. They take the time to research alternatives, determine quality, check compatibility, and make sure their purchase decision is a good one. They make a considered purchase.

This kind of considered buying is common in some business-to-consumer (B2C) segments such as automobiles, mortgages, wealth advisors, insurance, vacations, education, and so on. And considered buying is norm in most business-to-business (B2B) segments. The money involved is often larger, and the stakes of making a good or bad decision can be significantly higher.

Stalking the considered purchase has been the traditional domain of the sales professional—our lonely hunter out to bag a big one. Traditionally, salespeople, whether on a car lot, in a telephone boiler room, or in a designer suit and starched shirt, have been the vehicles through which buyers conducted their research, formed their preference, learned about price, and concluded a transaction. And this tradition sometimes meant that the deciding factor of who won a deal was based on which sales rep hosted the best three-martini lunch.

It's not that brands don't matter in considered buying. You've probably heard the saying, "no one ever lost their job by buying from IBM." And certainly brand names remain a driving factor in such important consumer segments as automotive, as they have for more than a century. But the truth is that brand is only a foot in the door for most considered buying. A large gap still exists between our lonely hunter having a respected brand to sell, and finding a specific quarry to stalk for dinner. This is where the cold call came in. Supported by air cover from a good brand, the sales rep remained largely on his own to find the prey.

Then a relatively new marketing function called "demand generation" stepped into this gap. Even though I've had a front row seat for this process in my 30 years as a manager and executive in Silicon Valley technology companies, I can't quite pinpoint when that term first emerged as the moniker for a function or group in the marketing department. But it's there now.

BIG DATA SPAWNS DEMAND GENERATION

If I think back to the 1980s, there was simply no demand generation team in the marketing group. Sure, marketing sometimes attended a trade show and came back with a handful of business cards that they'd hand off to the sales folks. But it wasn't really a profession, and it didn't have a name.

I can remember a big discussion that took place around the executive table at one of my companies in the early 1990s. The head of sales was complaining that his team didn't have enough deals to work on. So the head of marketing volunteered to hire a team of telemarketers to help make cold calls and find some leads for sales to work on. There was still no "Director of Demand Gen" at that time; it was just something that the corporate marketing folks did to try to be helpful.

Just as technology has been pivotal to the reinvention of both the manufacturing process and real-time supply chains, it has also been the indispensable catalyst in the emergence of demand gen as a marketing function. Its arrival coincided with a growing recognition of the "demand chain," as the less well-known but equally important counterpart to the "supply chain" in the overall business "value chain." Supply chains had already been reengineered and dramatically improved through the technology developments and innovative business practices noted in this book's introduction. Now the demand side of the business value equation was also ripe for reinvention.

The seeds that eventually grew into a formal demand generation function in the marketing department took root somewhere around the time of the developments noted earlier. That's when new technologies such as database marketing, data mining, and sales force automation (SFA)—later to be called customer relationship management (CRM)—started making their presence felt in business.

As with so many other nascent technologies, database marketing and sales force automation were expensive and complicated in those early years. They were so new and complex that companies needed specialists, often in the form of expensive consultants or agencies, to help figure out how to use them. But unlike their colleagues who focused on activities involving brand development, communications, and awareness building, the users of these tools emphasized lead generation and its associated metrics.

THE RISE OF "LEFT BRAIN" MARKETING

For most of its history, colleagues regarded marketing and marketers as being a bit fuzzy—using soft metrics, or often none at all—in crafting images, messages, brand promises, and promotional themes for their wares. Some of that was understandable; it really is hard to quantify what happens inside a customer's head. And the business contribution of feel-good messaging, while generally pleasant and almost always inoffensive, is difficult to justify at budget time.

The coming of age of digital media and associated customer targeting methods opened up new possibilities. Marketing departments could now start using data and analytics more easily and effectively. They could manage customer contact databases, deploy lead management programs, launch campaigns, and begin to measure their results.

At first, there wasn't much data available to use or measure. For all but the largest companies, data consisted of purchased lists of contact names for direct mail or telemarketing drives, and measurement was limited to counting contacts or responses.

Then everything changed. The mid-1990s saw the launch of AOL, the World Wide Web, e-mail, mobile phones, and new web directories like AltaVista and Yahoo! The availability of data exploded overnight in the suddenly interconnected worlds of media and marketing. We could track and count web visits, monitor and analyze e-mail clicks, and purchase, track, and test new online media such as banner ads.

Old-school, "right brain" creative marketing types, who more often than not had focused on brand, communications, and awareness-building, were generally not well suited to the new data- and analytics-driven activities in their abruptly changed world. They needed a new generation of "left brain" marketing specialists to fill this need—people comfortable with the number crunching, measurement, and technology that were at the heart of the demand gen function. "Left brainers" everywhere recognized the fast-growing opportunity and jumped into the business to manage new demand gen programs. Thus, a critical new marketing role was born: the demand generation professional.

The convergence of these changes led to a cultural shift in which corporations treated lead and demand generation as legitimate business functions and processes. Although people may not have seen it that way at the time, it was an historic shift in business strategy and management. Companies finally started to understand that they could improve and optimize the demand side of the value chain, just as they previously had with the supply chain, manufacturing, and finance functions.

It wasn't long before a new generation of demand gen professionals began to capitalize on emerging information and powerful new technologies to transform both marketing and sales. Even more significant, the rise of demand gen represented an historic shift in the way companies went about the business of creating, managing, and accelerating their revenue.

Today, the role of demand generation is well accepted among corporations as a distinctive and vital part of the marketing function, especially in B2B companies and others where the buyer makes a considered purchase. It is increasingly common to see a "Director of Demand Marketing" working alongside his or her counterparts who are responsible for managing such closely aligned departments as marketing communications and brand.

But all is not well in this new world. Yes, a new profession has emerged, featuring great tools, lots of data, and a celebration of left brain thinking inside the marketing team. It has led to a palpable sense among executive revenue leaders that an immense opportunity is waiting to be seized. It's obviously important to generate leads for sales, and one cannot overestimate the potential value of demand generation to business growth and success—but only if it is done correctly.

Advanced analytics can identify customer targets. Today's marketing professionals can use traditional (e.g., direct mail and telemarketing), new (e-mail), and even newer (search and social media) tools to contact target buyers. Then, once a prospective buyer responds to an outreach or piece of marketing content online, marketing can rightly say that it has created a valuable lead. Historically, it's been the hunter's job in sales to follow up on leads. So marketing's leads are promptly handed off to the sales team, where just about anything might happen. Unfortunately, that anything is usually not a sale.

KEY POINTS

- Different products and services require different marketing and sales approaches.

- Impulse buying may be common in consumer goods, but carefully considered purchases are the norm for B2B sales and many segments of B2C sales as well.

- Brand names matter for both consumers and businesses in considered purchases; however, they can only go so far in securing a sale.

- Demand generation as a distinct marketing function came as a result of having prospect data available, resulting from the use of new information technologies.

- Demand generation has made marketing a much more data-driven discipline.

- In order to capitalize on the opportunity presented by demand generation management, one must take a different approach to the sales-marketing interface.

CHAPTER 5

Sales Is from Mars, Marketing Is from Venus

Twenty years ago, a newly published self-help book by Dr. John Gray stormed the best-seller lists. *Men Are from Mars, Women Are from Venus: A Practical Guide for Improving Communication and Getting What You Want in Your Relationships* outlined the author's ideas about why it is such a struggle for so many men and women to meet each other's needs and develop more satisfying personal relationships. Whether the result of biology or culture, Gray explained, males and females often have different communication styles and modes of behavior. The failure to recognize and accept those differences leads to resentment, conflict, and an ultimately dysfunctional relationship. But how does this theory apply to business?

Picture this: Marketing runs a promotional campaign and hands over a stack of leads to sales. The sales team immediately dismisses them as poor quality and either demands better leads or simply ignores them and continues cold-calling. Potential leads go cold, marketing lead generation budgets are squandered, sales misses their quota, and nobody is happy. Sound familiar?

It's a scenario that is a lot more common in corporations today than many of us would care to admit. The fact is that communication problems between marketing and sales are often so fundamental and so persistent that in many cases their relationship can only be described as dysfunctional.

Frequent disagreements, competing objectives, misaligned compensation systems, and very different work styles cause marketing and sales to behave like bickering spouses in an unhappy marriage. Their dysfunction frequently expresses itself in petty grudges and exaggerated claims. "Sales never calls any of our leads," says marketing. "Those marketing leads are no good, why bother?" sales answers. "Our leads are golden! We worked hard to generate them," replies marketing. "Go back to your pretty colors and press releases and leave us alone," sales responds.

In my role as CEO at Marketo, I have frequently had the opportunity to talk with my peers and with revenue professionals in all kinds and sizes of companies around the globe. Since my company's business is all about transforming the way that marketing and sales teams work and collaborate, I am often treated like some sort of glorified marriage counselor. "Why can't my marketing and sales teams get along?" these business associates ask. "What can I do to break the log jam?" "I'm just so sick of the bickering."

CEOs and other executive leaders are more than just the long-suffering observers of this bickering; they are frequently part of the problem. Like an unpleasant mother-in-law (but unlike my own mother-in-law, I hasten to add), executive leaders often manage to throw little bombs into the mix that end up stoking the marketing and sales dysfunction. When CEOs want a revenue forecast, they intuitively ask their head of sales without even considering what their Chief Marketing Officer (CMO) might have to say about the topic. Chief Financial Officers (CFOs) talk about sales as the "revenue producing" part of the organization. They use words like "making investments in more salespeople." But when they refer to spending on marketing, they don't talk about it as "investments"; instead, they refer to costs, and questionable costs at that.

None of this is news to seasoned executives and managers. The strained relationship between marketing and sales has been around for about as long as there have been marketing and sales teams working together. Until recently, those strains have mostly served as a source of eye-rolling and irritation, but not really as a fundamental drag on business performance. But today, this dysfunction has metastasized to become the single greatest source of lost productivity and squandered revenue in the modern corporation.

There is a tremendous opportunity to improve this situation. Transforming this relationship into one of mutual respect—and more importantly, continuous collaboration among the best that both sides have to offer—can become a tremendous source of opportunity for top-line and bottom-line business performance and revenue growth.

Stop Talking to My Customers!

Your prospective buyers are out there, deciding where among competing alternatives to spend their money. They are researching, investigating, exploring, asking friends about your brand, your products, or your services. But one thing they are certainly not doing is spending any time at all worrying about how well your marketing and sales teams get along, or where one leaves off and the other picks up during the selling process.

The pot frequently boils over at the moment that marketing turns a lead over to sales. I have found that the top sales executive usually insists that marketing stop communicating with a prospect once sales accepts a lead and begins talking with a prospective buyer. This isn't just a routine request; it is an emotionally driven demand, rooted in mistrust and a deep conviction by sales that marketing will somehow "screw up" a deal cycle once the sales team is engaged. I've witnessed screaming matches between marketing and sales that occurred when this rule was violated. In fact, this is such an important, emotional, and widespread issue that we created a whole set of features specifically designed to allow our customers to implement these no-contact business rules in their companies when we first designed and built our lead management product at Marketo. I am sorry to report that many of our customers still actively use these features.

But I'm convinced that in essentially all of the buying cycles that involve a salesperson—whether it's inside sales, field sales, or a partner channel doesn't matter—your buyer will continue interacting with your marketing team *after* they've begun talking to your sales team. After all, even the customer's simple act of visiting your website constitutes an interaction between your buyer and your marketing team. And that's not all. Your sales rep doesn't really have much of a say as to whether your prospective buyer decides to attend a compelling webinar that your marketing team has produced. And because your buyers are in control, their interactions are likely to bounce between marketing and sales dozens of times over the course of a complex buying cycle.

Therefore, if your marketing and salespeople aren't working together as a single, seamless team when that buyer does bounce back and forth, your revenue team's dysfunctional relationship is likely to show through—to your competitive peril.

SOMETIMES OPPOSITES DON'T ATTRACT

Considering the number of dysfunctional marketing/sales relationships I have either observed first-hand or heard about from friends and colleagues, I've rarely actually met a marketing or sales professional who deserved to be part of this unfortunate drama. The truth is that most marketing professionals really do want to help sales be more successful. They understand that if sales wins, their company wins—and so they win. And they're great at what they do. Likewise, most salespeople work hard to make their numbers any way they can, and a lot of them are really awesome at the art of selling. Why then is this relationship the source of so much conflict?

The bottom line is that the marketing and sales professions are very different, and so they attract people with starkly different personality types. As we saw in Chapter 2, marketing departments emerged alongside sales teams. They were put there because they could complement the sales function by implementing ideas and strategies that applied to entire customer categories rather than just to individual customers.

Contrary to what many salespeople seem to believe, companies did not "invent" marketing departments to serve as vaguely irritating cost centers. But the jobs and personalities of great marketing and sales professionals are so distinct that their teams usually fail to understand what makes the other tick. They don't see what motivates the other, and they get little help in doing so from their executives, who also cannot recognize the potential for harmonizing the different personalities into a one-plus-one-equals-three type of equation.

REVENUE REVOLUTIONARIES

Craig Rosenberg, Vice President of Sales and Marketing, Focus.com

Focus is a network of thousands of leading business and technology experts. They are thought leaders and veteran practitioners, as well as upstart innovators representing a multitude of disciplines in hundreds of different markets. Through his work with this elite group, Craig Rosenberg has a front-row view of what is really happening—or not, as the case may be—in changing the marketing and sales functions to improve revenue performance. Here are some excerpts from a conversation I recently had with Craig:

> Ninety-five percent of all companies are completely dysfunctional in terms of their marketing and sales activities, even if they're succeeding at selling. I ran a panel at a sales conference where everyone was talking about how marketing and sales are finally starting to get together to work more collaboratively and be more effective. Several people pointed to the breakout success of a leading CRM company, and how it managed to crack the code in optimizing marketing and sales. But all the while I was thinking to myself that this isn't actually a great example. The fact is that when you are successful at selling a lot of stuff, you tend to overlook many things that are not working very well at the company—especially its revenue process, which is not usually treated as a real process.
>
> My experience has been that, more often than not, B2B organizations are completely dysfunctional in their ability to capture revenue. Even as you try to

(continued)

(continued)

help them meld their marketing and sales functions into a cohesive revenue chain, you realize that the dysfunction is all over the place. Very few companies seem to have the ability or foresight to take a step back and say, "well, let's look at this from start to finish and figure out where things are broken, and where they can be reengineered and optimized." The sales team realizes they have some issues and constraints, which are preventing them from making even more money. And marketing, even as it continues to push for more budget, still can't understand why sales isn't closing a hundred percent of their leads.

I do believe most marketing and sales executives realize there are real problems getting in the way of generating a lot more revenue. But, it's hard to make much progress because of this constant friction between marketing and sales. Changing this revenue equation, and drastically improving the sales-marketing alignment, is one of the biggest opportunities for businesses today.

Stereotypes can be risky, and there are always exceptions. But in this case, I think the classic stereotypes of marketers and salespeople include some valuable insights.

In general, salespeople are extraordinarily focused on achieving results right now. The best marketers, on the other hand, tend to focus on longer-term goals such as how their brands will be perceived months and years into the future. So they work on complex demand generation programs that can require months of advance planning.

The best salespeople tend to echo the wisdom of Wall Street's fictional Gordon Gekko: Greed is Good. To feed this greed, they'll extract resources from elsewhere in the company, and extract maximum revenue from customers. And while salespeople may need to become less like lone wolves, there is still an element in which they actually do need to act as solo entrepreneurs who tend to their sales territories. Marketing, on the other hand, is inherently a team sport. Sophisticated projects like producing a large trade show or user group meeting require coordinated teamwork across dozens of professionals. Salespeople tend to be risk takers; marketers tend to be thought provokers.

These differences are exacerbated when marketing feels like a second-class citizen, or that the sales department gets all the glory. Closing a deal provides a tangible reflection of sales' hard work and successful results. For marketing, on the other hand, it's a struggle to attribute any revenue to a well-honed image campaign that the department was responsible for generating.

The result is a tendency is for C-suite executives to view marketing as a "cost center," while characterizing sales as the "profit center." When you add to this uncomfortable mix such organizational issues as who "owns" leads, prospects, and customers, mutual mistrust between marketing and sales becomes rampant. It's no wonder marketing department heads often feel somewhat insecure.

TOWARD A MORE HARMONIOUS AND PRODUCTIVE RELATIONSHIP

It's not an easy task to encourage marketing and sales to communicate better, let alone see eye-to-eye and truly collaborate. But devoting time and attention to achieving this goal is far more than just a nice thing to do. It is imperative, and can be a major competitive advantage for your company, particularly since so few businesses get it right.

Jim Dickie, Managing Partner with CSO Insights, a research and consulting firm that specializes in helping companies improve marketing and sales alignment, sums up the problem this way: "I'm still shocked at the number of companies which do not even have a formally agreed-upon definition of what [makes a lead] sales-ready. The marketing team has its definition of what is marketing-ready. And the sales department has its own point of view on what constitutes a real opportunity. But there is typically a significant disconnect between the differing views, and that carries forward into continuous conflict at the boundary between marketing and sales."

The chapters ahead will outline a bold strategy for fundamentally transforming the sales-marketing relationship. It is an epic journey. But even the longest march starts with a single step. So to get you started, here are four small steps you can take that will point your marketing and sales teams in the right direction:

- *Focus on value delivered.* Educate marketing and sales team members on each other's contributions to your company's short- and long-term revenue growth. Hold regular, well-defined meetings where key marketing and sales executives identify shared obstacles, develop common revenue objectives, and set strategies for overcoming barriers to growth.

  Case in point: Wes Wasson, Senior Vice President and CMO of Citrix Systems, comments that his VP of Demand Generation also serves as part of the sales team staff: "He is as much a part of the sales team as my marketing organization. He attends all the sales meetings and seamlessly integrates his work with that of the sales group. At the same time, he owns allocation of the worldwide demand generation budget, which gives him an important level of control over what ultimately happens on the marketing side."

- *Agree on lead quality.* Have marketing and sales jointly determine what makes a good lead, and when that good lead is ready for sales. These definitions are crucial, as they're a frequent sore spot in the sales-marketing relationship. You must address them head-on in an atmosphere of shared responsibility and opportunity.

- *Take each other to work.* Try a "Take your colleague to work" initiative. Marketing should go or at least listen in on sales calls, and salespeople should regularly participate in meetings concerning marketing strategy and creative development. This sort of collaboration may sound incredibly self-evident, but it actually occurs way too rarely. My own company has made joint meetings and activities between marketing and sales a standard operating procedure.

- *Take them out for a beer.* You've heard the maxim "people buy from people." It's true. You must never lose sight of the fact that human relationships matter. While structured initiatives can begin to improve the alignment between your marketing and sales teams, salespeople and marketing people are, in the end, just people. And in many companies, the two don't mix very much. Sometimes it's because they sit in different buildings or states or countries, and sometimes it's just because they have quite different personalities and don't naturally socialize together. Find ways to encourage your marketing and sales teams to get to know each other, both at the management level, and the grass roots level. Sales may be from Mars and marketing from Venus, but every so often, a little bit of magic happens when you mix them together.

The key to building a healthy atmosphere of communication and cross-functional cooperation is to embrace the strengths of both your marketing and sales organizations. You will need to shift your organization's practice away from linear lead hand-offs and focus instead on mutual and shared accountability for lead generation, nurturing, conversion, and customer loyalty.

With a little work, and by following the suggestions outlined above, your marketing and sales teams will begin their journey toward a truly collaborative, symbiotic relationship that will turbo-charge your revenue growth engine.

KEY POINTS

- The relationship between marketing and sales is an unhappy one in many companies, much like a bad marriage.

- Transforming that relationship into a more respectful and productive one can be a source of tremendous opportunity for revenue growth.

- Many sales executives want marketing to get out of the way whenever a lead is handed off to them. However, that's usually not possible, because prospects continue having contact with marketing material, including websites and webinars.

- The tasks and personalities of career marketing and sales professionals are usually very different, which aggravates their differences and makes synergy more difficult to achieve.

- Initial steps toward improving the sales-marketing relationship include frequent meetings to define goals, create shared definitions for lead quality, and to get to know each other on human terms.

CHAPTER 6

The Sea Change Called Social Media

W hen did you finally realize that Facebook was more than just a flash in the pan? Was it when you starting receiving daily "friend" requests from people you hadn't heard from in years? Or when you literally couldn't avoid seeing something about Facebook in just about every news outlet on the planet? Perhaps it was when the reports started circulating that Facebook's valuation was approaching the stratospheric level, especially for a young private company, of nearly $100 billion? Or maybe it was when you found yourself wondering, "is it Winklevosses or Winklevii?"

How about Twitter? Do you remember when you went from having no clue about what a hashtag was, or why you should even care, to figuring out what hashtag to use for your upcoming family reunion or company user group meeting?

And what about LinkedIn? When did you first realize that you actually cared how many connections you had, and felt a twinge of pride that you had more than your boss? (Or was it jealousy when you realized that the hotshot on your team had more connections than you did?)

And Google+? If you're like me, it took about two days to go from sighing in wonder at why the world needed another social network, to busily organizing your circles and inviting your Facebook friends to join you there.

It has been less than a decade since any of these social media services started, yet in just that brief time they have become an inescapable and ubiquitous fact of daily life. They have also catalyzed the latest surge in high tech investments and initial public offerings (IPOs) and have become the subject of a mad scramble in marketing departments everywhere to figure out what it all means as the boss exhorts, "What are we doing about social?"

My 30 years in Silicon Valley have given me the ability to take a long view on social media. I have seen so many new technology cycles, hype cycles, and business cycles, that it is difficult for me to get too carried away with today's social media madness. Yet even with my admitted skepticism about irrationally exuberant trends in technology, I would argue that one cannot overestimate the huge impact that social media have had, and will continue to have, on business.

As I see it, the emergence of social media is just another part in the continuous evolution of technology interacting with the process of revenue creation. At the same time, it introduces a starkly disruptive change to that process.

First, let's look at why we can consider social media to legitimately be "more of the same," albeit a very important more of the same. I argue throughout this book that the most important trend affecting business today is the shift of power from sellers to buyers, and its resulting disruption of established marketing and sales practices. Social media are, in effect, just the next step in this transfer of power.

If you're old like I am, you may remember Usenet, and Gopher, and Archie, and Veronica (if you don't know what I'm talking about, feel proud that you're not a nerd). These services were some of the first examples of user-generated content, Internet directories, and search engines, well before the emergence of the World Wide Web. Back around 1991, when I was in the market for a new personal computer and trying to decide between an Amiga and a Macintosh, I distinctly remember asking people on Usenet and using Archie to search the pre-WWW Internet to help me make a buying decision.

My point here is not to take some odd trip down memory lane. It is instead to pinpoint this era as the pivotal moment when power began its irrevocable move from seller to buyer. I was able use these primitive Internet tools to learn far more about my purchase options than I ever could have, short of talking to a salesperson. I was an informed and empowered buyer by the time I finally bought my Amiga.

Since that moment 20 years ago, we have all seen this shift in power accelerate: first with the emergence of the web, then directories like Yahoo!, then Google and various specialized search engines, and now a vast array of other sites built around customer reviews and user-generated content.

Social media have seized on that shift and pushed the pedal to the metal. Today, extensive online networks of friends, associates, and people with shared knowledge and interests have given buyers a vastly expanded set of tools to research products, educate themselves, and make informed buying choices before ever talking to a salesperson.

POWER SHIFT

Make no mistake: The social media revolution constitutes more than just another step in the evolution of this power shift. It is really a qualitatively different beast, one with the ability to shift the power balance between buyer and seller more quickly and completely than all the previous technologies combined. As a result, social media have become the single biggest change agent the revenue process has ever experienced.

This new world in which buyers are mainly informed by social media is marked by transparency, authenticity, and agility. Accordingly, for anyone in sales or marketing, those qualities have now emerged as central to their hopes for success in brand building, marketing communications, campaign design, or sales.

Let's explore each.

TRANSPARENCY: IT'S ALL OUT THERE, SO DEAL WITH IT

I had a fascinating discussion during a meeting I recently attended with the head of marketing and sales for one of the world's largest makers of gas turbine power generators. He explained that their products are essentially big jet engines combined with generators that are used to provide emergency power to hospitals, data centers, and other critical resources during power outages. Then he asked my advice about an issue that was very much on his mind.

He told me that, until recently, his company had treated its price list with extreme confidentiality. They believed it was essential to their business, particularly since they had different price schedules for the same products depending on whether they were selling to hospitals, government, IT, or other industry segments. They saw pricing confidentiality as critical to maintaining their selling prices and maximizing their margins.

However, this company recently discovered—to their shock—that the street prices for their $25 million jet-engine-based generators were being shared on Twitter! So, much to my amazement, here's the question he asked me: "How can we stop this, and make our pricing confidential again?"

My answer recalled the famous Five Stages of Grief, where I pointed out that he and his company were still in the Denial phase over social media's impact. My advice was for him to get on with Anger, Bargaining, and Depression, so that they could quickly move on to Acceptance.

Acceptance, in this situation, meant coming to terms with the fact that social media are here to stay, and that customers would probably be comparing prices on Twitter from this point forward. Once he understood that, we could at least talk strategy—in terms of how to cope with and even exploit this change. I advised him to turn transparency into a virtue. If their prices were going to be public anyway, maybe they should think about building a brand image that highlighted their commitment to transparency, ease of access to critical buying information, and simplified procurement, since they didn't need to spend as much time negotiating price and terms.

AUTHENTICITY: CROWD-SOURCING THE TRUTH

In a world where buyers are isolated and have relatively little access to information, it's not hard to create a brand image or product positioning that's out of line with the "truth." Take, for example, a clothing company that introduces a new line built around a cool, hip, socially conscious image. Meanwhile, they're hiding the fact that they manufacture their clothes in a third-world sweatshop. In the not too distant past, unless you happened to read an exposé by an investigative journalist, there is little likelihood you would discover such an unpleasant truth.

One of the most profound and game-changing insights from social media is that the voice of the crowd really does discover and converge on the truth. No single individual necessarily starts with the whole picture, but by sharing and resharing, and discussing, and challenging, the crowd *will* figure out that the socially conscious brand is a sham.

In the business world, this means that the social crowd will figure out if a product has poor quality, a company is lousy at customer service, or a list price is different from the real selling price. This new world of information makes it essential that brands, product positioning, and marketing campaigns strive toward truth and authenticity. You're not going to pull the wool over the crowd's eyes, so don't even bother trying. Instead, embrace authenticity. In the same way that the crowd has an uncanny way of spotting lies and half-truths, the crowd can also identify if you're truly being genuine. And when they do, that positive word will get around just as rapidly and powerfully as all the negative 411 about sweatshops.

AGILITY: WHATEVER HAPPENS, IT WILL HAPPEN FAST

It is amazing how fast information spreads in the social world. If there's a flaw in your product, an error in a document, an unsettling government action, or a bold competitive move by a rival, it's likely that your prospects and customers will figure it out almost as soon as you do. It is therefore essential in this new information-saturated world for customer-facing teams to strive for unprecedented levels of agility in monitoring social media for breaking news, accepting and dealing with whatever good or bad news appears, deciding quickly how to respond, and leveraging the same social media channels to get your response back out right now.

But you cannot do all of this without software tools to assist in monitoring discussions about your company, its brand, and its products, or for coordinating a consistent and rapid response. But there's good news here: A new generation of easy-to-use, cost-effective social monitoring tools has emerged, and it's essential for every company to adopt and master these technologies. (And my company does not sell such tools, so this isn't a self-serving recommendation; it's survival advice.)

Finally, when you're in the thick of it, striving to respond quickly to whatever comes your way, don't forget to be transparent and authentic. An agile response that is less than candid could be worse than no response at all.

The bottom line is that it's hard for a company to hide anything when its good, bad, and ugly features are being shared ad infinitum on all sorts of social networking sites. I personally believe that in the end, greater transparency and authenticity will spur more competition, leading to better products and greater value for everyone concerned. This will be one of the most beneficial and enduring byproducts of social media.

Remember, though, that when you conduct your business in a social world with real authenticity and transparency, you are also at the same time transferring even more power and control to your prospects and customers. While this change is genuinely radical, it is also inevitable. Every company will have to learn to adapt to it. The best companies will not only adapt; they'll seize the moment by fundamentally reinventing their marketing and sales strategies to reflect this sea change in how to engage, nurture, and convert customer relationships.

KEY POINTS

- Social media have grown from nothing into a giant over a remarkably short time span. The giant's continued growth is unstoppable.

- Social media and the associated wisdom of crowds have introduced a major disruptive change into the revenue creation process.

- Information gathered from social media empowers buyers and accelerates the transfer of control from the seller to the buyer.

- As a result of the open communication that social media encourage, sellers must learn to embrace transparency, authenticity, and become agile in responding to breaking news.

CHAPTER 7

Coffee's Not Just for Closers Anymore

All of us know movies that have left such an indelible mark on the culture that people routinely quote from them. For example, most people who hear, "This one goes to eleven" don't need to be told that it's a line from one of my personal favorites, the 1984 classic *This Is Spinal Tap*.

It is therefore a testament to the mythic place the salesman holds in our collective psyche that one of the most quoted movies of all time, especially among sales types, is *Glengarry Glen Ross*, David Mamet's biting and mordant take on the sales profession. Of course, "profession" is too elegant a word to describe the job held by the Glengarry salesmen. "Racket" is probably more fitting for Mamet's outrageously cynical view of what really happens in sales.

Among the movie version's most famous lines is one delivered early in the film by Alec Baldwin, who plays a brutally condescending senior sales director giving his hapless uptown sales crew a pep talk—actually more of a do-or-die order—and does so brilliantly. Baldwin reminds the assembled group that he was sent on a "mission of mercy" from company owners "Mitch and Murray," who are located "downtown."

Early on in this darkly funny, but also kind of sad pep talk, the most down-on-his-luck salesman (played by Jack Lemmon) tries to grab a simple cup of coffee. The Baldwin sales manager pounces on him mercilessly, shouting, *"Put that coffee down! Coffee's for closers!"*

That one line captures the essence of the sales culture, both as we have come to know it and, too frequently, how we manage it. According to Mamet's familiar sales doctrine, if you can close the deal, you could win the sales contest and the proverbial Cadillac. If you can't, then even a cheap set of steak knives is probably too good for you. So don't pretend it's over until it's over.

In addition to being memorable, the "Coffee's for closers" line speaks to how sales continues to be viewed within the business context—the close is the ultimate triumph overshadowing all others. It reflects how out of touch so many businesses are in the way they see and manage their sales function.

Now, don't get me wrong. I am not denigrating the ability to close a sales deal, or the importance of using incentives to spur salespeople. However, the old model of doing whatever it takes to close the deal comes across as increasingly dated, if not plain wrong, in today's business environment. In the new world order of business, more often than not, buyers have neither the time nor the patience for the always-be-closing tactics that have traditionally won the day in sales.

The idea of a formal sales process is anathema to most of these sales VPs. For them, it's more about John Wayne-style heroics—the lone sheriff getting the job done, because that's the way it's always been. It is a sales mythology indelibly etched into the business consciousness, even at some of the world's biggest and most sophisticated companies. The Glengarry way does not change easily.

BIG CHANGE IS ALREADY HERE

Make no mistake about it: Real change is going to come. It's already here in the relationship between buyers and sellers, making corresponding changes in marketing and sales inevitable for any businesses that hope to compete effectively. Things simply work differently in this fast changing, technology-driven, global economy. Even in a tradition-bound profession like sales, larger forces eventually conspire to bring change forward, even if it arrives kicking and screaming. Just as the lone *High Noon* hero of yesteryear gave way to professional lawmen, the end-of-the-line sales hacks of *Glengarry Glen Ross* are being replaced by sophisticated, team-focused, socially savvy sales professionals using hot new technologies.

One of the most intriguing of those new technologies is the Apple iPad. A short few years ago, when it was first launched, people asked:

"Would anyone care? Would anyone even buy it?" Well, we now know the answers to those questions, and the iPad has become a runaway best seller.

But what is most surprising about the explosive popularity of Apple's iPad is how enthusiastically corporations, and especially sales departments, have embraced it. Upon launching the iPad 2 in the spring of 2011, Apple reported that 80 percent of Fortune 100 companies had already either tested or deployed the first version of the device, and that corporate adoption has continued to accelerate. It is now increasingly clear that Apple's pioneering tablet has emerged as a new standard for the sales professional, especially suitable for salespeople meeting with customers out in the field and on the road. For example, medical device leader Medtronic has issued more than 5,000 iPads to its sales reps. And technology giant SAP distributed 3,500 of the devices to its people. In addition, Mercedes put 400 iPads in its dealerships to keep their transactions on the showroom floor, right beside the actual vehicles.

THE END OF "TELLING AND SELLING"

The headlong corporate rush to iPads is striking on several fronts. Its touch-sensitive screen in place of a keyboard, while both trendy and attractive, is probably the least important of them. What is most significant to me is that the iPad signals a major shift in what businesses now expect from the portable computers they deploy and from their road warriors who carry them.

Think about the typical laptops that armies of salespeople carry. Why have companies invested so heavily in issuing tens of millions of laptops to their sales forces? The answer is easy: Companies want their people to be able to track prospects and have immediate access to key information in corporate CRM databases. Of course, they can also use those laptops to make presentations (the frequently derided PowerPoint deck) but the main business purpose is inputting, tracking, and managing data.

The conventional wisdom about the iPad is that it's great for consuming information, but not so great for capturing information. That argument was originally made by the technorati who proclaimed the new iPad to be mostly a consumer device. Indeed, everything about the iPad runs counter to the traditional case for using computers in the field, and no one can really say with a straight face that the iPad is ideal for plugging information into traditional enterprise applications.

The iPad's easy-to-handle form factor and elegant touch screen interface are tailor-made for consuming and relaying information in an effortless, interactive way. While its design is not optimized for entering lots of information or really for typing of any kind, companies and their salespeople are embracing iPads in a big way.

The reason for this is likely because of the way that the buying process has changed. Today's buyers can access valuable, relevant information online, especially through trusted sources on social networks, blogs, and communities of interest. They no longer need to engage the supplier company to do basic research. That leaves sales reps in a role that is more about communicating, educating, and helping the potential buyer. It is no longer just about telling, selling, and trying to close the prospect; it's about interacting on the buyers' own turf.

ENCOURAGING COLLABORATIVE COMMUNICATION

Here is where the power of the iPad and similar tablets come into play: As the relationship between the buyer and seller has changed, salespeople have had to adjust the way they approach the newly empowered buyer, and be in touch at precisely the right moment—whenever the buyer is ready. The iPad helps to break down old barriers, even the physical space of the buying situation, to enable better, more effective consultations.

All of these changes are part of a transformation in the ways companies create, manage, and accelerate revenue. The old business revenue paradigm has been broken for years. Forward-thinking companies are realizing this more and more, and are taking bold steps to transform their marketing and sales processes, metrics, and entire revenue-generating engines. Today, these corporations are beginning to look at their revenue demand chains in much the same way they did years ago when they reengineered their supply chains and manufacturing programs using breakthrough strategies such as Six Sigma and Total Quality Management.

The same is true at the individual level. Smart salespeople are starting to use similar strategies as they rethink their approach to the new buying/selling process. Now, at least, they have access to the same information their prospects have, which helps level the playing field.

This is probably also a major reason why more and more salespeople are jumping at the chance to use the less intrusive, highly mobile, user-friendly iPad: It engenders collaborative, consultative conversations with prospects. Being stuck talking to a prospect from behind a laptop has become very last-century to modern day sales superstars.

If history teaches us anything, it's that change does happen, whether we like it or not. That includes revolutions that come in all different guises, supported by many different tools. So if arming a sales organization with iPads or similar tablet devices provides the spark that helps ignite a revolution in the traditional marketing and sales process, it is truly a positive change for business.

Kirk Crenshaw, Vice President of Demand Generation at the cloud solutions provider Appirio, has helped to drive change in the roles of marketing and sales. As Kirk observed in a recent discussion:

> Traditionally, the sales department completely controlled everything—the information, and the whole purchase process. Of course, that has changed, especially because of the web. Buyers are now talking among themselves on social networking sites, sharing product experiences and information with their peers. The onus is on your marketing department to get as much information as possible into the hands of those prospective buyers, so you can educate them about who you are, and why your products and services are different and better. The last thing you should do is hide the information behind some registration page.
>
> When somebody ultimately does raise their hand, you need to have an understanding of what they've done in the past, where they've gone on your website, and what they've done to get to the point where they're making a decision to

contact you. Then you need to share that information with your sales team, and make sure they understand that individual's specific needs. The entire buying/selling process has changed, and you need an integrated marketing and sales approach to get the most out of it.

Who knows? If Jack Lemmon's character in *Glengarry Glen Ross* had been given an iPad to use on his evening "sits," he might have been able to buy his own coffee machine, one that even steams the milk for cappuccino.

KEY POINTS

- The always-be-closing" tactics of old-school salespeople don't work well with today's well-informed buyers.

- The acceptance of iPads by businesses for use by their field sales reps has significance beyond either data entry or the display of company presentations. They have become ideal collaborative tools that help salespeople to share information with their prospects.

- Marketing professionals are responsible for making as much useful information as possible available online, available to their sales colleagues and to prospective customers.

CHAPTER 8

A Research-Based Perspective on Superior Revenue Growth

When researching the ideas presented in this book, I wanted to find out which kinds of marketing and sales best practices companies with superior revenue growth shared in common. So I commissioned a survey in which we asked more than 100 top executives from public companies how they ran their marketing and sales functions. Their responses provided a number of key insights into the marketing and sales practices associated with sustainable revenue growth.

As part of the survey, we asked executives about their experience, revenue management practices, and marketing and sales spend patterns, as well as specific practices such as marketing metrics, lead management, and technology adoption. In addition to examining the specific results for each question, our research team used a multiple regression model to see if combinations of practices correlated with the critical question of revenue growth.

Based on the survey responses, we found that high-growth companies were more likely to have the following characteristics:

- They have relatively experienced sales executives, yet comparatively younger and less experienced marketing executives.
- They spend more on marketing as a percentage of revenue, with the best spending at least $.50 on marketing for every $1 spent on sales.
- The companies' top marketing and sales leaders discuss revenue directly with the CEO, either together or separately.
- The most senior sales leader typically reports to the Chief Operating Officer (COO) rather than the CEO.

The following sections will explore the significance of these findings in more detail.

EXPERIENCE VERSUS FRESH EYES

Let's start by examining the differences in the two types of executives themselves. Figure 8.1 shows an interesting insight: High-growth

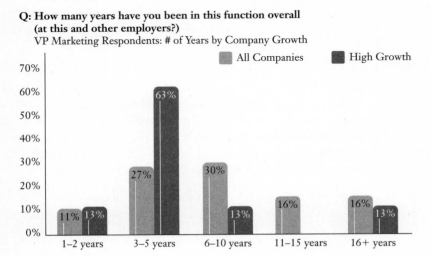

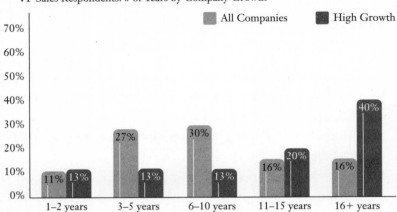

FIGURE 8.1   Marketing appears to value fresh eyes and new experiences, while sales conversely appears to put a premium on long job tenure.

companies employ seasoned top sales leaders with 16 or more years of experience in that role. By contrast, top marketing leaders at these same companies are newer to their jobs; most only have three to five years of experience in the top seat.

It seems that the best way to excel in sales leadership is to have a lot of experience actually selling. Conversely, senior marketing executives should bring a broader set of experiences and fresher, more constantly renewed perspectives to their work. In some ways, this comes as no surprise; digital technologies have not yet completely disrupted the traditional sales process. But marketing hasn't been able to avoid disruption from search engines, social media, and myriad other digital marketing technologies.

HIGH GROWTH MEANS A HIGHER MARKETING PERCENTAGE

From the marketing and sales spending information provided by the respondents, the survey also saw a correlation between the rates of revenue growth and the percent of revenue spent on marketing. Figure 8.2 shows that higher growth companies spend 3 to 4 percent of their

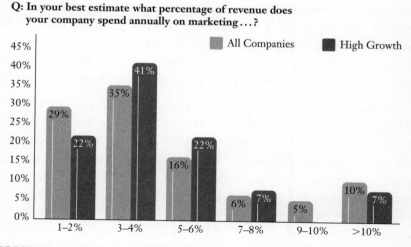

Q: In your best estimate what percentage of revenue does your company spend annually on marketing...?

FIGURE 8.2   Companies that spend proportionately more on marketing tend to achieve higher growth.

revenue or more on marketing, instead of the 1 to 2 percent that many companies currently spend.

Beyond that, high growth companies tend to spend at least $.50 on marketing for every dollar spent on sales. This means that companies not only need to have a baseline of marketing activity in place, but their sales efforts become more effective when they're supported by more marketing investments. On the other hand, revenue growth declines if a company over-invests in sales to the point where it outruns marketing.

This suggests that corporations should consider reapportioning their marketing and sales budgets in order to boost revenue growth. They should allocate more for their marketing staff and programs, rather than just pouring more money into hiring additional salespeople.

This probably sounds counterintuitive; it certainly runs counter to established dogma in corporate marketing and sales. But of course, that's the point of this entire book: We must disrupt our old, dysfunctional ideas about what works in marketing and sales.

COORDINATED MANAGEMENT OF MARKETING AND SALES MATTERS

Left to their own devices, marketing and sales departments simply won't align themselves. Yet as I pointed out earlier, companies need better internal alignment to accelerate revenue growth. Three of the characteristics we found in our survey suggest just how important it is to coordinate marketing and sales to achieve superior revenue growth. But doing so requires management time, attention, focus, and metrics.

First, the CEO must hold both marketing and sales accountable, and more closely use equitable metrics for each to determine individual advancement and compensation. However, the survey found that in terms of daily operations, it's desirable to have a reporting structure through which the company's operational management devotes direct attention to marketing and sales. As shown in Figure 8.3, companies with higher growth rates tend to have their head of sales and head of marketing report to the COO—that is, to a more operationally focused executive—than to the CEO. We explore marketing and sales reporting relationships in more detail in Chapter 25.

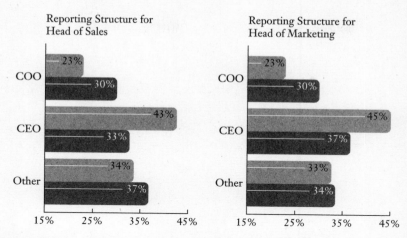

FIGURE 8.3   Companies tend to grow faster when the head of sales and the head of marketing report to an operationally focused executive.

KEY POINTS

High-Revenue Growth Companies

- Have relatively more experienced sales executives, and comparatively younger, less experienced marketing executives.

- Spend more on marketing as a percentage of revenue.

- Have top marketing and sales leaders who discuss revenue directly with the CEO.

- Have the most senior sales leader typically reporting to the COO rather than the CEO.

CHAPTER 9

Leaving Trillions on the Table

I hope I have made at least one point abundantly clear in Part I of this book: In order to continue to prosper in today's radically altered buying environment, corporations need to make equally radical changes in their marketing and sales strategies. This is truly a change-or-die scenario for senior corporate executives wondering how to spur revenue growth and profitability (and I can't think of any who are not).

To achieve breakout revenue growth, businesses need to transform every aspect of how they create revenue. They must rethink the roles, responsibilities, metrics, and processes that are used by their departments on the front line of revenue creation, specifically marketing and sales. In the same way that Six Sigma became the shorthand name for the transformation of manufacturing excellence and quality, I call the strategies needed for revenue transformation Revenue Performance Management, or RPM.

I've tried to explain over the past eight chapters why companies must transform their revenue generating structures to thrive in this newly interconnected world. The remainder of this book will explain how all companies, no matter their size, can actually achieve breakout growth.

Before we embark on the rest of our journey, let me make clear the stakes that are on the table. I recently led a global study to quantify the bottom-line impact of transforming a company's marketing and sales activities through RPM. The study, conducted in 2011 by Marketo's in-house research team, calculated that by adopting RPM, businesses worldwide have the potential to bring in a total of $2.5 trillion—that's trillion with a "t"—more in aggregate revenues by 2017 than they had at the time of the study. These findings confirm the virtually unlimited opportunity that RPM can offer for revenue acceleration; some customers even reported 40 percent or more in revenue growth after they adopted a comprehensive Revenue Performance Management strategy.

REVENUE REVOLUTIONARIES

Zuora

Zuora is the global leader in subscription commerce and billing, a company that helps organizations in every industry transition to the Subscription Economy. Clients use Zuora's multi-tenant cloud-based platform to launch, scale, and monetize their subscription services. Zuora's applications work where traditional Enterprise Resource Planning (ERP) applications fail, particularly in subscription pricing, quoting, orders, billing, payments, and renewals. Zuora was an early adopter of RPM as a primary driver of its business growth and market leadership.

CHALLENGES

While planning to launch Zuora back in late 2007, the company's founders realized that the market into which they wanted to sell was both huge and complex. It included a variety of verticals that had varying needs and business practices. It also involved different target customer roles that they needed to address appropriately; one-size-fits-all marketing simply wouldn't work. At the same time, their sales process had to include multiple touch-points that they would organize, time, and optimize in order to achieve maximum results.

The Zuora marketing and sales team wanted to establish their company's visibility in the sales funnel from the front end, to the marketing-qualified lead phase, and then onto the sales-qualified lead level. Their challenge was to use this process and the entire revenue cycle to focus their sales professionals on the highest probability leads; at the same time, they had to ensure that they responded in a timely and intelligent manner. The company also realized that they needed a marketing platform specifically built to handle the complex sales and marketing tasks they needed to perform. In Zuora's view, other marketing automation offerings on the market were designed as single-purpose platforms, and were therefore insufficient for the company's ambitious revenue management and scalability needs.

SOLUTION

To meet its full range of sales and marketing needs, Zuora worked with Marketo to implement a complete RPM solution that would synch with the company's established salesforce .com infrastructure. This allowed Zuora to effectively manage its total revenue cycle, from high-volume automated demand generation campaigns all the way down to closing sales.

During every step of the RPM process, Zuora relied on Marketo software and expert support to track contacts, rate prospects, and measure the return on investment (ROI) for every marketing campaign. Doing so involved simultaneously managing 15 to 20 marketing outreach campaigns, scoring leads in the revenue cycle, and nurturing prospects until they were ready to hand over to the sales team for closing.

BENEFITS

Zuora now manages massive amounts of data, drives multiple campaigns simultaneously, and measures each marketing effort's ROI. In the process, they can supervise every stage of its revenue cycle funnel and focus on prospects and opportunities that deliver the greatest revenue. Marketo's RPM solutions have also enabled Zuora to strengthen the integration of its marketing and sales activities in order to optimize the entire revenue generating process.

(*continued*)

(*continued*)

The ultimate proof is in Zuora's sales results after implementing Revenue Performance Management. By using RPM to build a higher-powered revenue engine, Zuora has continued to grow sales and revenues by 400 percent year over year. In the past 18 months alone, Zuora closed 10 deals worth more than $1 million each. At the same time, the company has also doubled in size to nearly 200 employees.

Jeff Yoshimura, Zuora's VP of Marketing, says, "Just as Zuora is enabling the transformative Subscription Economy, Revenue Performance Management is empowering companies to transform their sales and marketing processes and achieve truly breakout revenue results."

The study we conducted at Marketo also found that the accelerated revenue growth that companies achieve by using RPM is not the result of any single factor. Instead, measurable improvements in business performance result from a systematic approach to transforming a company's marketing and sales processes across the full buying cycle. When taken in combination, they produce such eye-popping results as the 40 percent revenue growth statistic cited above. Examples of key quantitative improvements in revenue processes identified by the study include:

- 46 percent increase in the number of real buying opportunities available to the sales team.

- 12 percent improvement in average contract value.

- 17 percent improvement in sales win rate.

- 15 percent reduction in total customer acquisition costs, allowing more resources to be invested in growth.

There is indeed "real money" available for companies deploying RPM. It is an approach to reengineering the marketing and sales demand chain that can transform the entire revenue process in a major way. In the coming chapters, I will lay out a roadmap and action plan you can use to capitalize on this trillion-dollar revenue growth opportunity.

KEY POINTS

- It has become imperative to transform a company's sales-marketing strategies in the current business environment.

- Revenue Performance Management, or RPM, provides a set of strategies leading to such a transformation.

- An aggregate $2.5 trillion in potential new revenue is available to companies that adopt RPM strategies.

- The synergy of systematic process transformation, more than any single element of it, is responsible for improved results.

- Improvements include increases in sales opportunities, contract value, win rates, and customer acquisition costs.

PART II

THE ROAD TO REVOLUTION

Transforming the Revenue Model

CHAPTER 10

The First, Crucial Step
Committing to Fundamental Change

We are living, marketing, and selling in a brave new world, one where buyers determine their own brand preferences, research their own alternatives, ask friends about vendor qualifications, learn about pricing, and consent to talk to a salesperson only on their own timeline and terms. We have seen how this new mode of buying has run headlong into hidebound marketing and sales practices that have not really changed much over the past 50 years. This clash of styles has created an enormous challenge for companies everywhere. But we have also seen the promise: Companies that embark on fundamental change in the ways they create revenue have the opportunity to unleash a radically higher performance revenue channel, take share from competitors, and achieve outsized revenue acceleration of 40 percent or more.

The issue is real. The opportunity is huge. The strategy is concrete and actionable. Yet we all know that change is hard, even when we know it's change for the better. Otherwise, we wouldn't have Jenny Craig and Nutrisystem and Lean Cuisine all helping us lose weight; we wouldn't have SmokeEnders and Nicorette gum and QuitNet to help us stop smoking; and we wouldn't have over 262,000 self-help books available from Amazon.com.

However, as with so many other aspirations for change and improvement in our lives, we sometimes need both a carrot and a stick to spur us into action. Just as the threat of heart disease can motivate a diet or fear of lung cancer prompts you to quit smoking, the alternative to fundamentally transforming your bad business habits related to creating, managing, and accelerating revenue is equally daunting. Companies that fail to embark on revenue transformation are doomed to waste resources and suffer underperforming sales, brand erosion, and loss of share to more motivated competitors.

So let me begin Part II of this book with a Manifesto for Revenue Change—a call for change in virtually every aspect of the way you manage marketing and sales at your company, your department, or in your own job. To ease our way into it, let's look at how radical change in a corporate context can pay off.

THE VALUE OF REAL CHANGE

Business history is rich with standout examples of forward-thinking business leaders who embraced and drove change. They had the foresight as well as the fortitude to recognize rapidly shifting realities—in this case, where the buyer has taken control of the selling process—and then leveraged emerging technologies to create new business methods and innovative products to achieve outsized growth.

In fact, it's the winners who always get out in front of change. They don't wait until altered realities have forced their hand. Instead, they are already reading the tea leaves, looking for signs of macro trends buffeting their businesses, and seeking opportunities to improve, even when they think things are going pretty well at the moment. They're the ones who say, "If it ain't broke, then break it anyway."

Even massive global companies like IBM make change a core part of their culture and business strategy. IBM, which recently celebrated its 100th anniversary, opted for a transformation after a near-death experience back in the late 1980s. The company had become caught in the classic market leader trap, which is a persistent danger for large, successful companies that enjoy huge business results from their legacy of leadership. As one of the earliest technology pioneers, IBM helped to create the original computer industry. And for years, they reaped the benefits of market leadership by turning in consistent revenue growth and soaring profits. Life was good for Big Blue and its shareholders.

But nothing lasts forever, especially in technology. Even as the bluest of blue-chips, IBM found itself tossed back on its heels when the growth of its mainframe business, the company's historical sweet spot, started to decline, as the market shifted elsewhere (as it eventually will for any business). Under the disruptive leadership of new CEO Lou Gerstner during the mid-1990s, IBM performed a 180-degree change in its corporate strategy, shifting a significant portion of its business away from hardware and toward global software and services.

This fundamental shift was credited with saving IBM and putting it squarely back on the road to future growth and success. Since that time, the company has thrived by driving continuous change in its various business lines. Recently retired CEO Sam Palmisano faced his own existential challenge around the time of the 2001 recession. Rather than simply trying to survive the economic downturn, Palmisano launched his own effort to transform IBM into what he termed the "globally connected enterprise." His new strategy stood in stark contrast to IBM's previous approach, which had been built around a classic multinational structure with its national businesses coordinated by a global headquarters.

In its "World in 2011" issue, *The Economist* called IBM and other companies like it *multinationimbles*. The magazine commented that the "big winners will be companies that can combine the advantages of scale with the agility to respond to fast-changing market conditions." It predicted that in 2011, "Some of the most venerable incumbents will show the world they have figured out how to do creative destruction themselves."

I believe that the biggest and best target of opportunity for creative destruction for many companies is their current marketing and sales process.

THE IMPERATIVE FOR GROWTH

The past three years or so have witnessed the bleakest business climate of many of our lifetimes. Jobs and budgets have been cut, often to the bone, as companies have looked to weather the "Great Recession" and its aftereffects. Yet companies both large and small are coming around to an inescapable conclusion: that you can't slash yourself into long-term success any more than you can diet yourself into a muscle building championship. Instead, the direction is simple: *Reigniting revenue growth is the business imperative of the day and of the decade.*

Growth may be imperative, but it's naïve to assert that costs no longer matter. We must both drive revenue growth and continuously improve profitability from that growth. Of course, this process is easier said than done and achieving it requires smart investments in resources, plus a fundamentally different game plan for growth than the one that many organizations applied during the first decade of the new millennium.

It's hard to fault corporate executives for hesitating to invest again in today's business climate. The fact is, however, that the smartest companies create opportunity out of turmoil. Many are already moving aggressively ahead with strategies for growth ignition in the competitive times ahead.

A 2011 survey from The Conference Board, a premier global business research firm, underscored the increasing importance of growth as a strategic imperative for corporations worldwide. According to the results of their *CEO Challenge 2011* survey, CEOs across the globe cite the most critical challenge they face as business growth. More than 700 CEOs, presidents, and chairmen from different geographies and industries participated in this study and, according to The Conference Board's CEO Jonathan Spector, "The global CEO consensus about 2011 suggests that growing one's business is the key to success," he said. "Now more than ever, business leaders are turning to new ideas, products, and markets to fuel growth, drive innovation, and remain competitive on the global stage."

DRIVING GROWTH BY CHANGING THE MARKETING AND SALES DYNAMIC

Corporate executives who want to fuel growth are increasingly asking themselves: "How do we move forward intelligently? Where do we go from here?" They sense that big changes and real opportunities are afoot for companies who have the courage to seize the moment, overcome the challenges of the status quo, and capitalize on change.

As discussed in the first part of this book, the revenue-creating parts of the modern corporation—the marketing and sales departments—embody fundamentally different crafts and have strikingly distinct cultures. Marketing tends to be more creative, thinking longer-term, managing brand identity and programs that span weeks, months, or even years. And frankly, marketing can also be a bit soft in terms of how it approaches the world. Marketing executives tend to focus too much on the qualitative dimension, often getting so caught up in words, pictures, and messages that they fail to focus on hard performance metrics and bottom-line ROI.

Sales, on the other hand, is the ultimate "what have you done for me lately" organization. Salespeople are trained to think and perform to optimize for the extreme short term: "How do we get the deal across the finish line . . . now?" A salesperson or team might work a deal for a long period of time, but it is still all about "going for the kill" and getting the deal done as soon as possible.

The contrasting psychologies, personalities, and cultures of marketing and sales personnel can seriously impede the goal of driving increased revenue. This is especially so in a world where the buyer is in control, and where essentially all buying starts on the web and in social media. The fact is that buyers complete 60 to 70 percent of their research and decision-making before a salesperson ever contacts them. This hard truth does not leave much room for maneuvering without fundamentally rethinking marketing and sales processes you use internally to create revenue.

Newly empowered prospective buyers have told us in no uncertain terms that they couldn't care less about this rift between marketing and sales. The buyer is simply searching for basic necessities to do her/his job: information, service, and a great price. At its most basic, they want, and increasingly demand, their needs to be met in a seamless fashion across the channels owned by marketing, such as the website, product collateral, or social media, and those channels owned by sales, including the phone call, 1:1 web demonstrations, and so forth.

Changing this dynamic opens the opportunity to ignite revenue growth. The first payoff comes when marketing and sales become so aligned that they're able to engage together with the buyer on the buyer's terms. That's when marketing begins to see itself as an integral part of the revenue equation, and accepts revenue-driven quotas and success-based compensation plans. They also agree to be measured based on hard results such as the flow of genuinely qualified leads to their colleagues in sales. Marketing is able to fulfill these commitments because they own the early stage of the buyer process, and can use the best of web, social media, and marketing automation technologies to capture and develop leads that the sales team values.

The second payoff happens when sales starts to act on and value the leads that their marketing colleagues deliver. If a sales team can shift its allocation of time, even just a little bit, away from cold calling and early-stage prospect development and toward competitive differentiation, value selling, and closing business, then overall sales efficiency immediately increases. And the results of increased sales efficiency drop straight to the bottom line.

The third payoff takes place when marketing and sales are able to truly collaborate around a common process that features shared metrics and definitions. To this day, many companies continue to waste an amazing amount of time arguing about what is, and is not, a good lead. Their definitions are all over the map. There is no common vocabulary, and few common terms between the marketing and sales camps. And you simply cannot make real progress together if you're not able to communicate clearly, effectively, and consistently.

Finally, the last and arguably most important payoff is the Big Picture story. This comes when organization members can understand, analyze, optimize, and forecast the entire revenue funnel—from early-stage social engagement to closing revenue—as part of a single, coherent process. At this stage, the heads of marketing, sales, and finance, along with planning professionals, general managers, and CEOs, are all able to work from a common view of the revenue process. As a result, they're all able to gain more visibility into future revenue performance and allocate strategic corporate investments in revenue to wherever they'll have the highest return.

TIME TO COMMIT TO FUNDAMENTAL CHANGE

There are dozens of points at which one can study, measure, and optimize the revenue creation process. But it's first essential to grasp the central idea that revenue generation is not just something sales does.

It is an entire process with the same complexity, sophistication, and nuance as many better understood business processes like manufacturing, supply chain, or even quote-to-cash.

The next few chapters will lay out an entirely new way to think about marketing and sales. I hope it will encourage you to make changes in the way you create, manage, and accelerate revenue growth at your own company.

KEY POINTS

- The dysfunctional state of revenue creation today is evident in countless industries' poor marketing and sales performance.

- Successful companies look for signs of emerging trends that could affect their business—either for better or for worse—and then act on them.

- The most promising target for creative destruction is today's dysfunctional marketing and sales model.

- Revenue growth is the business imperative of this decade.

- The payoffs from implementing an improved marketing and sales model include a clearer, more complete, more actionable view of the entire revenue process.

CHAPTER 11

Is Revenue the Weakest Link in the Chain?

A chain, as the adage goes, is only as strong as its weakest link. Over the past few decades, virtually every link in the business process—from supply chain, to finance, operations, product development, and even human resources—has been reengineered and improved by application of sophisticated management strategies.

But there's one major exception: the *demand chain*—that is, those business processes that encompass everything a company does that involves marketing and sales. Now it's time to reinvent the demand chain as well, since doing so will fundamentally improve the way businesses create and grow their most important asset: revenue.

All other core business processes that underwent fundamental transformations have resulted in improved efficiency, quality, and contributions to profitability. In the 1980s, there was Six Sigma. In the 1990s, it was Supply Chain Management. In the early years of the 2000s, there was Agile Development. This book's call to adopt Revenue Performance Management (RPM) will do for revenue what earlier process transformations have accomplished for other key business functions.

Professor Michael Porter of the Harvard Business School pioneered thinking around the corporate value chain approach, claiming that this method "disaggregates the firm into its strategically relevant activities in order to understand the costs and existing potential sources of differentiation." Figure 11.1 illustrates Porter's insights about the corporate value chain and its sub-parts, the supply chain and the demand chain. It shows how the value chain categorizes the generic

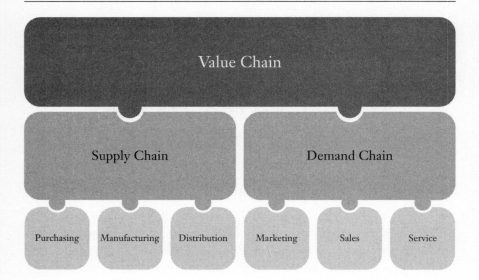

FIGURE 11.1   Michael Porter introduced the concept of the corporate value chain, spanning all of the activities that a product passes through from concept to market.

value-adding activities of an organization. Products pass through all these activities of the chain in order and gain some value at each activity.

The past 30-plus years have seen major transformations on the supply chain side of the picture. Companies have been able to make supply chains quicker, cheaper, and more predictable, primarily by applying advances in technology, Six Sigma, and other quality improvement programs to strip away inefficiencies. As a result, lean businesses have increased their productivity, saving billions, possibly even trillions, through just-in-time inventories, speed-to-market processes, and so forth.

On the other hand, progress toward improving performance and productivity in the demand chain has occurred at a glacial pace, largely flying under the radar of management gurus and corporate executives alike, even as the business and technology landscape has radically changed around them. It's ironic that such an essential component of every business's very existence should be able to lie low for so long.

I have a theory about why this might be the case. In their own ways, both marketing and sales are frequently viewed as "arts," and are therefore less amenable to process thinking, quantitative methods, and optimization than other parts of the business. Indeed, there is a true art to marketing: Crafting a powerful, transparent, and authentic brand; pricing and positioning to out-maneuver the competition; and communicating with and educating customers in a compelling and trusted way. And there is a true art to sales as well: Aligning with the buyer; qualifying and qualifying again; overcoming objections; negotiating a win-win deal; and bagging the quarry in the end. These arts are real, and must never be lost when bringing process thinking to the demand chain.

But the fact that there is some art involved isn't a reason to abandon improving the science and business parts of this process. RPM's goal is to bring this same degree process thinking to end-to-end revenue creation and to achieve the same level of improvement in business productivity and profitability that other process initiatives have delivered in the past. And, the best news is, the gains in productivity and profitability from implementing RPM come as the result of real and sustained top-line revenue growth in the business.

LEARNING FROM THE SIX SIGMA REVOLUTION

Six Sigma, a practice initially formulated by Motorola to improve manufacturing processes and eliminate defects, didn't emerge until more than 100 years after the dawn of the Industrial Revolution. But it worked remarkably well. In addition to substantially decreasing product flaws, it produced an unexpected benefit: It actually reduced the company's costs rather than increasing them, as many had expected it would.

During the 1980s, other business operations began adapting the Six Sigma approach. Corporate leaders realized that if Six Sigma worked so well for manufacturing, there were probably better ways of conducting and managing other of their company's key business activities as well.

There's an equally historic opportunity today to accelerate the shift to a much more productive and powerful revenue generating process on the demand chain side of business. We can apply one critical lesson learned from Six Sigma: Even though it fundamentally transformed many business processes, it never required the drastic step of shutting down a company's existing factories in order to build new ones. Instead, think of Six Sigma as a journey that involves continuously improving, measuring change, and always looking for new opportunities to recalibrate and further improve efficiencies and results. It requires that companies adopt a change in the company's business and operating culture, one focused on achieving continuously expanded value over time.

Reengineering the demand chain is also a journey. Along the way, we seek to build on what the best salespeople and the best marketers already do very well, and then give them the structure, strategies, tools, and methodologies to empower even greater success.

Like Six Sigma, Revenue Performance Management requires continuous measurement and tracking to drive improvement at every point along the demand chain. This is not simply about reorganization, a new job title, a new piece of software, or using new metrics. It is about embracing change, and adopting big ideas that improve the way we create, measure, manage, and accelerate revenue.

This journey to reengineer the demand chain is neither generic nor off the shelf. To succeed, it must always meet the individual organization's specific needs. It should also reward the outstanding work of those marketing and salespeople who join together in reinventing their company's revenue processes and it must celebrate their joint successes.

CONTINUOUS IMPROVEMENT IN THE DEMAND CHAIN

Revenue Performance Management is both the strategy and the process corporations use to transform the way their marketing and sales teams work—and work together—to accelerate predictable revenue performance. It can only be achieved through executive and organizational commitment, and a discipline of continuous improvement.

Using Six Sigma methods, and by adopting other transformation strategies of similar scope and impact, businesses have embraced the fundamental idea of measurement, adjustment, and continuous improvement. These ideas apply equally to the demand chain as well, and promise a whole new generation of improvements in business performance. By adopting RPM to measure and continuously improve revenue performance, corporations can increase marketing and sales effectiveness (revenue performance) and efficiency (cost reductions) in ways that go directly to the top and bottom line of the corporation.

The revenue chain will no longer be viewed as the corporation's weakest link.

Key Points

- Over the past 30 years, most key business processes have been reengineered to improve their effectiveness, efficiency, and contributions to revenue.

- Six Sigma and similar continuous improvement disciplines have been used as the basis for implementing these changes.

- Six Sigma is disruptive but not destructive; companies can transition incrementally toward its full adoption without suspending operations.

- Revenue Performance Management is to the demand chain and revenue side of the business what Six Sigma has been to the company's other key processes.

CHAPTER 12

The Power of a Revenue Cycle Process

O kay, you've decided to take the plunge and transform your traditional marketing and sales activities into a continuously improving, higher-performing revenue machine. Where do you start? The first step along that journey is to understand the different process components that go into creating revenue—what I will refer to here as the *revenue cycle*.[1]

If I had used the term "sales cycle," most people would have a pretty clear picture of what I was talking about. The sales cycle represents the steps involved, and time required, for a salesperson to close a deal. Most business leaders would say that a sales cycle runs from the moment a salesperson begins to talk to a prospective buyer, to the day he or she finally closes the deal. Sales cycles are usually divided up into phases or steps often called "pipeline stages," each of which has its own definition. Sales leaders use those definitions to assist in sales forecasting and deal management. There's a whole body of literature, as well as a bunch of sales methodologies, which have grown up around the concept of the sales cycle and pipeline stage management.

---

[1] In choosing to refer to the end-to-end process of creating revenue as a "revenue cycle," I want to acknowledge that this term has a very specific existing meaning in the context of the healthcare delivery industry in the United States, where "revenue cycle" refers to the complete set of processes from patient enrollment to billing for medical visits, to insurance management, to cash collection. I chose to use the term, despite this established meaning, because the analogy to the well-understood term "sales cycle" is too powerful to ignore. I apologize in advance if I confuse any healthcare revenue professionals among my readers.

Most C-level executives spend an inordinate amount of time thinking and talking about sales cycles and how they impact their sales pipelines. No doubt these discussions help, to some extent, with improving sales effectiveness and forecast accuracy. But it's really difficult to think about any of these sales cycle methodologies as being a true business process—at least not in the sense that you would talk about a manufacturing quality process, or a supply chain inventory management process, or a finance team's quarterly close process. That's because most executives with revenue responsibility are conditioned to think about sales as an art.

The very idea of sales reps conforming to a disciplined process is one they're inclined to laugh off, especially in light of the lone-wolf personalities who populate their sales teams.

As a result, most companies treat the measurement, analysis, and continuous improvement of the sales process as a quixotic goal. To be sure, the sales department is very precisely measured, especially in terms of top line revenue production. But all too often, the seeming clarity of this ultimate measurement has dissuaded revenue leaders from looking very carefully inside the box of the sales process. You don't want to set formal performance goals for the intermediate stages of the sales process that might risk messing up the final result. And even the minority of revenue leaders who do look inside that sales box almost always miss the mark.

REVENUE REVOLUTIONARIES

Jeff Ernst, Principal Analyst, Forrester Research, Inc.

Forrester Research is widely regarded for its expertise in sales and marketing. In its seminal report on sales and marketing alignment, Principal Analyst Jeff Ernst of Forrester captures perfectly both the problem and the solution. Here are a few key excerpts from the report, titled "B2B Marketing and Sales Alignment Starts with The Customer."[2]

---

[2]"B2B Marketing and Sales Alignment Starts with The Customer," Forrester Research, Inc., January 27, 2011.

Sales and marketing leaders are going about it wrong. To overcome the obstacles to alignment, they need to challenge conventional wisdom. Rather than relying solely on the point-to-point integration approach where marketing and sales teams participate in each other's meetings, these two groups need to align their activities around a common design point, which is the buyer's needs and problem-solving process [Figure 12.1].

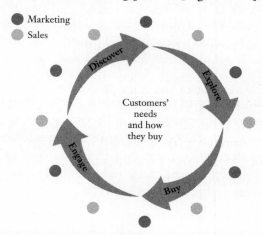

FIGURE 12.1 Marketing and Sales Align with Customers' Needs and How They Buy.
Source: Forrester Research, Inc. Used with permission.

The report continues:

The gap between marketing and sales didn't get as much notice when the economy was booming and even mediocre players in sales were hitting their quotas. But now:

- **The CEO is demanding accountability**. The challenges companies face in achieving revenue targets has made alignment between marketing and sales a high priority for the chief executive officer (CEO) (see Figure 12.2). There are fewer opportunities,

(continued)

(continued)

and prospects have tighter budgets. So it's harder than ever to generate high-quality leads and advance them through the marketing and sales process. Senior executives are holding marketing leaders more accountable for contribution to pipeline and revenue.

- **B2B buyer behavior has changed.** Buyers are often more than two-thirds of the way through their problem-solving cycle before they engage with a supplier's sales department. By the time they interact with salespeople, they demand more detailed information and expertise, which requires marketing and sales to deliver a well-orchestrated buyer experience.

- **The marketplace is getting more complex.** At the same time, everything is becoming more complex— product portfolios, customer requirements, competitive alternatives, and ever-changing market dynamics. Salespeople need more help than ever to reach their quotas and perform effectively.

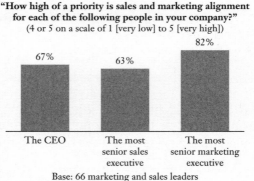

"How high of a priority is sales and marketing alignment for each of the following people in your company?"
(4 or 5 on a scale of 1 [very low] to 5 [very high])

Base: 66 marketing and sales leaders
Source: October 2010 Marketing And Sales Alignment Survey

FIGURE 12.2 Marketing and Sales Alignment Is a CEO Priority.
Source: Forrester Research, Inc. Used with permission.

Jeff addresses some other inconvenient truths for marketing professionals separately in the 2011 Forrester Research report: "Thought Leadership: The Next Wave of Differentiation in B2B Marketing."[3] In it, he explains that marketing leaders looking for a sustainable way to differentiate their company and offerings in the marketplace need to embrace thought leadership marketing because of several factors they don't like to admit.

- **Buyers don't care about your product.** When we asked business buyers what differentiates a vendor from its competition, the top three responses pertained to how the vendor solves the buyer's specific needs. Customers don't "buy" your product; they "buy into" your approach to solving their problem. Buyers seek out experts whose perspectives on the problems they face and approaches for solving them align with their own. Thought leadership puts your firm's points of view out there for prospects and customers to see.

- **Your products are commodities.** Companies typically market the features and benefits of their products and services, but feature advantages can be quickly copied by competitors. Thought leadership marketing allows you to put bold, new ideas into the marketplace, which attracts buyers and creates an affinity with your firm, making it harder for competitors to gain mindshare.

- **Your salespeople get involved in deals when it is too late in the process.** Sales leaders we talk with tell us that if one of their reps gets involved with a prospect after the request for proposal (RFP) is issued, they are usually too late, as another firm likely influenced the requirements to align with the strengths of their offerings. Marketing and sales teams need to engage buyers at the earliest points in their problem-solving process, when the need is identified. Thought leadership enables your salespeople to make the customer smarter, which increases your firm's presence as a potential solution provider.

---

[3]"Thought Leadership: The Next Wave of Differentiation in B2B Marketing," Forrester Research, Inc., June 7, 2011.

THERE'S MORE TO THE REVENUE CYCLE STORY

This book explains that today's buyer is indisputably in control of his or her own learning process, from the earliest stages of research through to the final purchase. They carry this process out on their own terms and their own timeline. Virtually every buying engagement nowadays starts with a web search, a question posed in one of the social media networks, or a similar interaction with a different prospective vendor. This means that buyers first interact with information resources and programs managed by the vendor's marketing team.

Therefore, virtually every revenue cycle starts with the marketing department; only later does it find its way over to the sales team. A salesperson might think they've initiated a sales cycle by placing a cold call; however, the buyer has almost certainly been primed to take the call as a result of his or her earlier interaction with a website, an ad, or some other marketing-sponsored activity.

Viewed through the buyer's eyes, it's easy to see why the notion of a sales cycle is a seriously flawed way of understanding how revenue gets created. After all, to the buyer the start of a sales cycle is simply an arbitrary point somewhere in the middle of their buying process. And there is no good reason for the seller to think that the activities that take place after this arbitrary point are somehow more important to the revenue process than those that happened earlier. In fact, as we'll explore a little later, the activities that take place prior to the arbitrary start of the sales cycle may actually be the most impactful in growing revenue efficiency and top line revenue results.

This is why instead of an arbitrary cycle that picks up somewhere in the middle of the buyer's journey, the RPM methodology calls for a comprehensive "Revenue Cycle Model" that captures every step along their way. This comprehensive model begins radically earlier in the process, when the buyer first registers any nascent impression of your company, your brand, and your products or services. It then continues through stages of building awareness, positive brand impression, anonymous self-directed research by the prospect, passing through qualified lead stages, and then finally on into the traditional sales cycle. Figure 12.3 illustrates a simple Revenue Cycle Model. The design and dynamics of the Revenue Cycle Model are discussed in much more detail in Chapter 15.

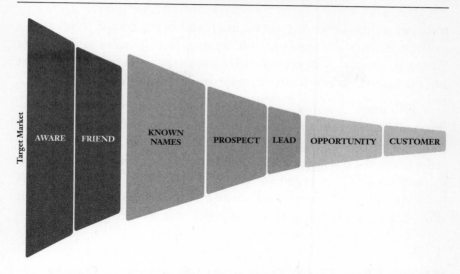

FIGURE 12.3   A Revenue Cycle Model captures each step in the buying process, from early awareness to closed customer.

Barry Trailer, Managing Partner of CSO Insights, a research firm focused on sales and marketing, puts the revenue cycle into perspective: "Instead of looking at the traditional roles of marketing and sales, we should step back for a moment and look at the entire revenue generating process. What does a holistic view of that process really look like? Where there used to be a bright line between marketing (pre-pipeline) and sales (in pipeline), now there is a fuzzy area of overlap. Marketing is still playing a lead role before the prospect ever enters the pipeline, throughout the revenue process. We also see sales getting involved a little earlier in the process than they're normally given credit for."

Barry continues: "The development of a combined marketing and sales revenue cycle funnel—one that flows only sales-ready leads—is the foundation of a high performance revenue engine. However, that new revenue engine only runs properly in companies where marketing and sales executives are effectively aligned and contributing to the sales process in a shared fashion."

Once organizations understand and model the revenue process as a seamless continuum spanning marketing and sales, they can identify key metrics to capture and analyze. That data can help a company better understand how its revenue creation processes are performing today, as well as how they can be improved in the future. With access to these metrics, it's then possible to start identifying what I call the "levers of change"—aspects of their business processes that companies can manipulate to accelerate revenue growth and efficiency.

Of course, companies of different sizes and in different industries will have significant variations in their end-to-end revenue cycles. But the model's key characteristics will be the same; it will accurately reflect how the buying process touches both marketing and sales from the earliest phase of brand awareness through to the closed sale and beyond. And it will include objectively defined steps and metrics that allow companies to measure and improve revenue performance.

WATER MAY FLOW DOWNHILL, BUT LEADS DON'T

The notion of a sales funnel has been around for decades. It provides a graphic and easily understood illustration of the sales cycle steps I discussed earlier in this chapter. As a result, the metaphor of a funnel has become ubiquitous among sales professionals. In it, each step or stage is a little smaller than the one before it, reflecting attrition—the idea that prospective buyers "fall out" as they progress through the sales process. Typically, sales funnels are shown flowing left to right or, more frequently, top to bottom so they look like real kitchen funnels. And illustrations of them often include a great big arrow that points toward the ultimate sale at the end.

Whenever I pour water through a funnel in my kitchen at home, it works just that way; water flows into the top and comes out the bottom. My funnel at home might as well have a big arrow painted on it. But here I'll let you in on a little secret: Despite decades of experts drawing essentially the same diagram, it turns out that revenue funnels don't really work that way. And this mismatch between the traditional sales funnel diagram and customers' real world behavior is one of the greatest sources of waste and inefficiency in the revenue process today.

It's easy to see why the funnel metaphor doesn't really make sense when you consider the real world buying process. To paraphrase the bumper sticker: Stuff Happens. Buyers begin to engage in a process and start talking to a salesperson, but might suddenly lose their budget. Or their boss quits. Or they quit. Or the government imposes a regulation that changes the business outlook for their company. Or their mother goes into the hospital. Or a competitor makes a move that freezes a market. Or a CEO suddenly changes priorities. I could go on and on with examples of interrupted buying cycles. They happen all the time.

The trouble with the traditional funnel model, with its big arrow pointing in just one direction, is that it fails to take into account those real world interruptions and variations in actual buying behavior. It assumes that a prospective buyer either gets to the end—whether as a newly closed customer or a lost deal, or that the buyer falls out somewhere along the way. The one-way funnel makes no provision for a prospective buyer whose budget goes on hold for two quarters or for a prospect who needs to look after an ailing mother for a few months. Instead, when an event like that happens, potentially promising leads just quietly disappear into the ether, leaving the appropriately greedy and short-term focused salesperson to move on to the next best lead. The very nature of the funnel, with each step smaller than the last, even seems to suggest that this is the way things are supposed to happen!

Of course, evaporating leads—prospects that just disappear, with no real accounting for where they went or why—are the bane of every senior sales executive's and CEO's and CFO's existence. Depending on the company and its industry, an advanced-stage sales lead might represent an invested expense of $1,000, $5,000, or more. If it were a laptop computer of that value, it would probably carry an asset tag and be tracked by IT throughout its useful life. Yet high-value leads regularly fade into oblivion, taking thousands of invested dollars along with them.

In the real world, the budget that was frozen for two quarters sometimes comes back to life. Many mothers get better and come home from the hospital. And priorities sometimes shift back to where they were before. In each of these cases, a disappearing lead may suddenly revive and point to an active buyer once again. And keep one thing in mind: just because you or your salespeople have forgotten about this prospect and moved on to the next best one, it doesn't mean your competitors have. The result: a deal that was there to be won turns into a silent and sadly lost opportunity, with all the time and resources invested being squandered.

The complete, end-to-end Revenue Cycle Model of Revenue Performance Management changes this picture completely. One of the key business processes to grow out of RPM is "lead recycling," wherein stalled leads are automatically returned to an earlier stage of the funnel. Recycling is complemented by a "lead nurturing" process, which maintains continuous contact and engagement with all leads, including recycled ones, so that whenever the buyer is ready to reengage, you're ready to pick up where you left off.

The big one-way arrow is erased in a Revenue Cycle Model; leads move up and down and back and forth throughout the process. They go from being owned by sales back to being owned by marketing, and then back again. Leads may opt out of further contact, or be lost to a competitor, or removed for many other reasons, but they never just get lost. We will explore these processes, and the benefits that result, in much more detail in Part III of this book.

KEY POINTS

- Sales cycles are often depicted as stages in a pipeline that represent the buyers' progression from awareness to sale.

- Most sales executives are wary of using disciplined sales processes that could conflict with the art of successful selling.

- Revenue cycles typically begin with buyers encountering information provided by marketing; sales cycles begin at the point of a prospect's first contact with sales.

- The initiation point for a sales cycle is arbitrary and usually in the middle, rather than at the start, of the buyer's journey.

- The sales funnel concept is widely used, but it is seriously misleading in several important respects, particularly including temporary obstacles experienced by buyers.

- The Revenue Cycle Model used with Revenue Performance Management does a better job of accounting for what is frequently a non-linear buyer's journey.

CHAPTER **13**

Marketing Is Not a Cost Center . . . It Is an Investment in Growth

---

Conventional wisdom, at least within the business community, sees a company's sales organization at the heart of where revenue is created. It is therefore often treated with deference. However, that's not the case with marketing. Instead of being seen as an integral part of the revenue process and an essential investment in growth, marketing is frequently considered to be a cost center—a dark hole into which dollars are thrown and from which decorative artwork sometimes emerges. It's easy to see why that perception persists, even to this day.

The number one topic of discussion at executive staff and board meetings is almost never the upcoming marketing campaign or new brand strategy; it's the last quarter's numbers or the next quarter's sales forecast. The head of sales invariably leads the discussion with little or no input from the Chief Marketing Officer. So it's no wonder most executives think of marketing as a cost center and not a central part of the revenue team.

My colleague, Jon Miller, the VP of Demand Marketing at Marketo, has observed that "when it comes to building credibility, marketing is its own worst enemy." Sadly enough, he has a point. Marketing executives too often sound like creative types when it comes to communicating with fellow executives, especially those from the C-suite. Of course, there's nothing wrong with being creative; it is an important part of marketing and business in general. It's just that CFOs tend to be more left-brained and focused on bottom-line results.

"Even the language marketing people use tends to position their function as a cost center," Jon continued. "We use terms like 'cost-per-prospect' and 'budget for a trade show.' Those words frame our actions in terms of costs that go out the door, when in reality they are investments critical to generating new revenue. The more that marketers can adopt the language and terminology that CFOs use, the more credibility we're going to have at the senior management table. Why not talk about critical business topics such as revenue performance, investments, ROI, gross margin, and profit and cash flow? Don't be the 'artsy craftsy' team perceived as a cost center; be seen as a key part of the company's revenue team."

Who Is in Charge of Your Company's Revenue?

In most businesses where there's a direct or indirect sales force that's responsible for all or part of the company's revenue, its sales department owns the revenue pipeline. Marketing may play a supporting role by supplying leads, although in practice, their leads are often ignored. Sales controls the revenue process and is held accountable for top-line growth. As a result, sales tends to hold more political power than any other corporate function. That's almost certainly why so many CEOs come from the ranks of sales departments.

Marketing, on the other hand, is usually excluded from the revenue process. At many companies, the sales team conducts a weekly revenue call where various sales leaders update their forecasts for the month or quarter, thus helping executive leaders keep their finger on the pulse of revenue. Yet nobody from marketing is even on the line. Over the past few years, I have asked literally dozens of senior sales executives, CEOs, and CFOs one simple question about their revenue call process: "Do you have your head of marketing in on the call?"

Amazingly, at least to me, almost no one answers with a simple "no." Instead, they look at me as if I had grown a third head and am spouting crazy talk. They start figuring out how they can get past me to the door.

Okay, maybe I'm exaggerating just a bit, but my point stands. Many executives cannot even fathom the notion that a marketing leader would be an integral part of the firm's revenue forecasting process. Instead, they see marketing as sort of a necessary evil, not a strategic asset that drives growth. Others may even question whether it's necessary at all. As one marketer lamented in a recent CMO Council report, "My group is perceived by upper management as the people who do color brochures."

Susanne Lyons has held CMO and general management positions at some of the world's best-known and most respected brands, including Visa USA and Charles Schwab & Co., so she has a unique perspective on marketing's role in the corporate scheme of things. "Back when I started in the business, marketing was such a subjective world, particularly brand marketing and advertising. The truth is that, in the past, it was very hard to measure the results and ROI of those marketing programs. The marketing goals that were set were too often soft and squishy."

"I remember having to push my marketing colleagues to make their metrics more quantifiable, and more tied to bottom-line revenue results. I also tried to make sure we had joint goals with the sales team. For us, it was never just a matter of creating clever ad campaigns and shooting out a bunch of brochures. But that was exactly how the marketing department's primary function was perceived," she added.

REVENUE REVOLUTIONARIES

Christine Crandell, Outside the Box Blog, Forbes.com

Some of the best writing I have seen on the growing revenue revolution is from Christine Crandell, who writes the excellent *Outside the Box* blog on *Forbes.com* and is president of NBS Consulting Group. I recently spoke with Christine about the challenges to revenue growth.

Phil Fernandez: It seems as though companies talk a lot about growth goals, but fail to deliver. What do you think is going on?

Christine Crandell: Every CEO has growth at the top of their agenda. But the economy is still struggling, so it's a huge challenge to achieve that growth. As I see it, though, one of the primary reasons it's so hard for B2B companies to grow is that

(continued)

(continued)

they're out of step with the way their customers actually buy. They're reading from different scripts. It's like trying to win *Dancing with the Stars* while you and your partner are following different dance routines. You're not going to win, and you're likely to step on your partner's feet.

PF: *Why do you think that is?*

CC: One major culprit is the misalignment of marketing and sales. Those two groups have never been able to work well together. I saw a recent Forrester Research report that said only 8 percent of all companies have actually aligned their marketing and sales. A somewhat larger group, 14 percent, has gone as far as to define rules of engagement for the way marketing and sales should interact. So it's no wonder most dance partners can't get their routines straight.

But you can also see that misalignment as a symptom of a larger, more systemic problem: Most companies really don't understand the journey that their buyers take *before* they finally sign on the dotted line. And for most buyers, those journeys have changed during just the last three years. Most marketing and sales types like to focus on their past experience when they're predicting future outcomes. But today's buyers see most sales encounters as a waste of time. So the question that marketing and sales leaders *should* be asking is, "How do buyers really go about buying?"

PF: *Is that actually happening?*

CC: Not really. When a company's sales numbers come up light, its CEO, sales, and marketing leaders typically blame each other. But if they could just step back for a moment, I think they could see what's actually going on. They would then realize that in order to drive growth, both marketing and sales need to align themselves with the buyer's journey, proactively manage the customer's experiences. Buyers expect consistency in the ways they interact with the brand for as long as they use the product, no matter the medium in which those interactions take place. Consistency is essential to building credibility with buyers, and it needs to extend beyond the initial purchase to include service and support as well.

There's an old adage I'm fond of that says "what got you to where you are today isn't enough to get you to where you need to be tomorrow." That may be even more the case today than when it was written last century. And it means that marketing and salespeople must get their act into line with the buyer's journey—the way buyers actually think and behave today—if they're ever going to deliver on growth.

TAKE A PAGE (OR TWO) FROM THE SALES PLAYBOOK

Many marketing teams today are suffering a crisis of credibility, since they're not considered as essential contributors to the top line. But it doesn't have to be that way. Marketers can offset these perceptions by framing their spending and results using such hard metrics as return-on-investment, revenue yield, and growth. Marketing budgets need to include revenue forecasts, and marketing plans need business cases that illustrate how they will drive revenue. Only by demonstrating how their efforts directly support revenue will marketers be seen as integral to the revenue process, and not a cost center.

Marketing professionals are usually great at positioning, establishing brand identity, and infusing excitement into their company's products. Those skills turned outward toward consumers are essential. Unfortunately, many marketers attempt to turn these same skills inward, toward their colleagues and executive managers; they try to hype their contributions to revenue, rather than to calmly measure and account for them. The results often sound hollow to other executives, including the sales leaders who are accountable for hard, visible metrics. Left unchecked, this tendency can marginalize marketing, rather than empower it.

So what can marketers do to ensure that executives see them as part of the machine that drives revenue and profits, instead of as people who create websites and buy tchotchkes? The key is to act more like sales, at least when it comes to creating, talking about, and being truly accountable for revenue. Taking these actions from the sales department playbook can help marketing professionals become as closely tied to revenue as the sales department already is.

- *Forecast Results, Not Spending.* Marketers must forecast leads, predict pipeline, and estimate revenue with confidence. This task is too important to be handled by sales alone, simply because marketing has information that sales doesn't—information that can increase the depth and accuracy of revenue forecasting. When the two groups collaborate and base their planning around one agreed-upon Revenue Cycle Model using a single set of metrics, marketing has the ability to "flip on the high beams" and look earlier in the funnel to estimate future revenue. For instance, marketing can use revenue analytics to predict how many new qualified leads will enter the revenue cycle funnel, how they'll move through the funnel, and how many of them will become "sales-ready" during any given quarter. In turn, sales must be able to forecast how many of those deals they can close and convert to revenue.

- *Make Hard Business Cases for Spending.* With the revenue forecast in place, marketing needs to make a solid business case for the resources required to deliver on those forecasts. This means knowing what it takes in terms of money, time, and effort to acquire and nurture qualified leads until they're ready to talk with sales. Marketers who use rigorous methodologies to plan their spending are better able to justify and defend their budgets. If the CEO wants to cut spending on marketing by 10 percent, the CMO can tell him exactly what impact that will have on next quarter's revenue. The reverse is true as well: By understanding the marginal return of incremental spending, the CMO can justify a larger budget and know exactly where to put the extra funds.

- *Employ a Formalized Marketing Methodology.* Sales departments usually have a well-developed playbook of methods to train new sales reps, identify ways to out-maneuver the competition, improve chances for closing deals, and assist with forecasting. Marketing groups therefore need the same kind of rigorous processes. I hope that this book will become one of the foundations in building that sort of disciplined thinking within the marketing profession. The use of a documented, formalized methodology brings two main benefits:

  1. First, it provides a common language that facilitates more consistent communication both inside and outside the department. Consistency is critical for reliable rollups and forecasts, as well as for accurate comparisons of value between different leads and opportunities.

  2. Second, a formal methodology improves performance by helping every marketer to perform more like the top practitioners in their field, regardless of their experience in using any given tactic or channel.

- *Use Marketing Metrics That Matter to the CEO and CFO.* Soft metrics like brand awareness, impressions, organic search rankings, satisfaction, and PR media hits are all important, but only to the extent that they eventually connect in a quantifiable way to hard metrics like pipeline, revenue, and profit. The marketing dashboard needs to track the impact of all marketing activities, whether hard or soft. By speaking the same quantitative language as the CEO and CFO, CMOs can more clearly communicate marketing's value and impact. As more customer interaction channels become targetable and measurable—and as marketing spend shifts to those channels—marketers will find it easier to measure the impact of marketing using hard analytics instead of merely guessing.

- *Demand Compensation Tied to Revenue and Objectives.* Sales organizations have credibility in almost every company. That's because, at the end of the day, they can't escape being held accountable for revenue; the monthly or quarterly quota attainment chart doesn't lie. And everyone knows that sales compensation is highly risk-based; salespeople really don't eat unless they make the kill. Marketing leaders must embrace this same philosophy if they are ever going to earn a seat at the revenue table. They have to set hard and measurable revenue targets in consultation with the CEO, CFO, and sales leadership. And then they have to put their necks on the line. The single best thing a marketing executive can do to earn immediate revenue credibility is to demand a more leveraged compensation plan—one involving less base salary and more incentive compensation tied to revenue—and then stand behind his or her numbers.

WINNING HEARTS AND MINDS

It is possible to change the longstanding perception of marketing as a cost center rather than an essential revenue driver, but it will take work. Marketing professionals need to master processes for making concrete revenue forecasts, treating spending as investments with committed returns and results, and speaking in terms of concrete business metrics like pipeline, revenue, and cash flow.

At the same time, marketing needs to be assertive. Marketing executives need to insist that their sales colleagues come to the table and begin to coordinate activities as a true revenue team. To facilitate these interactions, marketing needs to demonstrate in both action and word that they, too, are accountable for revenue performance. Also, since better accountability necessitates better performance, marketing needs to live up to its promises by delivering more leads and higher quality leads to sales as part of an overall Revenue Performance Management Process.

In Part III of this book, I'll delve more into specific levers that marketers, and their counterparts in sales, can pull to start revolutionizing their companies' revenue performance and drive outsized revenue results.

KEY POINTS

- Marketing is frequently seen and dismissed as a cost center rather than as a revenue generator.

- To offset that perception and bring marketing's true potential to the business, marketers need to speak the language of revenue and employ hard metrics.

- Neither corporate sales nor marketing people are particularly well tuned to their buyer's journey on the road to making purchase decisions, which often results in significant lost opportunities.

- To earn a seat of respect at the corporate table, marketing needs to adopt some of the practices used by sales—forecasting results, making solid business cases, using metrics that matter, and adopting leveraged compensation plans tied to revenue.

PART III

THE LEVERS TO REVENUE TRANSFORMATION

CHAPTER 14

People and Process; Art and Science

The first part of this book described how today's buyers are in firm control of the buying process, as well as how marketing and sales have grown up as disconnected departments, neither of which is well aligned with this new buying paradigm. I also explained how, in aggregate, companies can add *trillions* to their revenue by adopting a new transformative strategy called Revenue Performance Management, or RPM. Part II then outlined the principles guiding that transformation and introduced the Revenue Cycle Model, which provides a conceptual basis for understanding, guiding, and measuring the process of continuous improvement.

Now, it's time to get practical.

In order to successfully implement RPM, the entire company, from the top down, must embrace transformation. Everyone involved has to adopt and master a number of new or changed business methods. Changes in buying behavior have been abrupt, and it can be somewhat disorienting to people in marketing and sales. Every revenue professional today knows that the status quo is not going to work for them much longer; however, they don't quite know where to go from here. No one taught them new Revenue Performance Management methods in school. And, as we saw in Chapter 2, there are still plenty of well-respected training specialists, clinging to obsolete ideas and methods, who are teaching anyone who will listen all the wrong ways to succeed in this new world.

Fortunately, a number of forward-looking companies have spotted the opportunities lurking behind these changes. They've pioneered entirely new ways of finding prospective buyers, engaging them in a compelling discovery and evaluation process, and getting them to the proverbial "yes." They have begun to figure out and implement new marketing and sales methods. And they have started to remold their organizations, adopt new metrics, and update compensation practices to positively reinforce those changes.

At the same time, a new community of thought leaders and consultants has come forward to shape these ideas into formalized methodologies resulting in a set of relatively standardized terms and methods. Finally, a new generation of cloud-based software companies has emerged to deliver the business systems needed, both to support marketing and sales in this new buyer-centric world, and also to offer the analytics required to prove value and support continuous revenue performance improvement.

In short, all the necessary pieces are now in place so that every company, regardless of size or industry, can embark on a Revenue Performance Management journey. So let's go!

TOWARD A REVENUE MACHINE

If there is one central theme running through all the evolution-ary changes involved with RPM, it is this: Every company needs to design and build a high performance revenue machine. In the same way that centuries of artisan production gave way almost overnight to the Industrial Revolution, assembly line manufacturing, and scientific methods applied to business management, now the traditional arts of marketing and sales must yield to a repeatable, scalable, measurable, and increasingly efficient revenue assembly line.

Think about the characteristics of a modern high-performance machine—a sports car, a jet turbine, a semiconductor fab lab, an iPad, or whatever. In every case, specialists with expert scientific and engineer-ing knowledge labor with care to plan, design, and build the machine to precise tolerances. They build mockups, create computer simula-tions, and construct test beds to explore what works and what doesn't. They measure performance, identify improvements, and reduce costs, sometimes to the point that companies can account for tenths of a cent

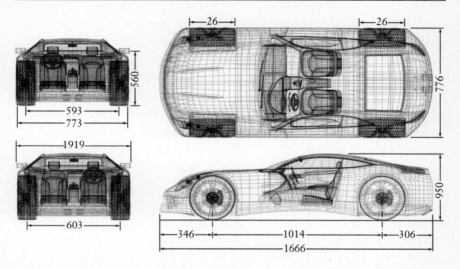

FIGURE 14.1   A high-performance machine starts with a great design.
Source: iStockphoto. Used with permission.

per unit in their manufacturing process. These same ideas apply to building a high-performance revenue machine.

How do we design a high performance, high efficiency revenue machine? The first step is to create a great design, one that sets the foundation for everything else that follows. We call that design the Revenue Cycle Model.

The Revenue Cycle Model details each step in the process of creating revenue, starting from the earliest stage, where a prospective buyer is just learning about your brand and products, and on through a series of subsequent steps that could span weeks, months, or even years. It continues to the moment when a salesperson earns the deal, and even beyond that, through the full customer lifecycle.

Just as the design for a high-performance machine includes specifications and goals (think: "this baby needs a top speed of 180 MPH, and highway fuel economy of at least 35 MPG"), the Revenue Cycle Model sets out specific details and measurable goals for revenue creation, so every step in creating revenue is well understood and designed to perform well.

The first step in revenue generation—meeting prospective customers at the start of their buying process—is a numbers game for most companies. Marketing must generate the highest possible number of potential leads. In a world where the buyer is in control, marketing's primary goal is to *be found* by prospective customers who are out looking. This is essentially the reverse of the traditional and much less efficient model in which marketing and salespeople play some sort of blind man's bluff trying to find prospects. When marketing people think about how to be found, they typically use key metrics like the number of *new, unique names collected per month or per quarter*, and the *cost per new name*. And the more names they get, the better their chances of winning the game. We will ultimately see as we tune our high-performance machine how math and statistics can be used to project future revenue on the basis of these metrics.

The game changes once a prospect becomes known to the vendor. Now, marketing's mission is to nurture every new buyer relationship, build brand recognition and affinity, support each buyer's individual research needs, and continuously keep track of everyone so that no one gets accidentally lost or forgotten. This is where the idea of *inventory* comes into play—that is, the inventory of prospective buyers working their way through their own individual buying processes.

These are the middle steps of the buying process, where the key metrics resemble those used in managing a company's work-in-process (WIP) inventory in a manufacturing supply chain. They include things like *average age of prospect relationship*, or *conversion rate to sales opportunity*. But unlike manufacturing processes, where having too much WIP can be bad, the goal of RPM is to *increase* the inventory of prospective buyers while ensuring that the inventory of buyers stays fresh and keeps moving at an appropriate pace.

If you cut to the chase, the next step in the revenue process is to separate the "lookie loos" from the real buyers. You have hit pay dirt if you can accurately predict which prospective buyers are most likely to actually make a purchase in the near future.

If you successfully navigate this hurdle, you'll reach the final step in the revenue process: closing business and putting revenue on the board. The objective here is to focus your expensive sales team's time and attention on the most likely buyers. If sales professionals can shift even a small percentage of their time away from cold calling, prospecting, or talking to unlikely buyers and instead spend that time working with motivated buyers, you'll dramatically increase efficiency and revenue achievement.

Each of the steps outlined here is a repeatable, measurable activity, one that can be designed, monitored, measured, and tuned through an ongoing process of continuous improvement. These steps are the cogs and wheels of your high-performance revenue machine. We'll explore in much more detail how to design and build them in the next few chapters.

"DANGER, WILL ROBINSON"

The mechanistic view that I articulate here can be disturbing for executives, managers, and professional practitioners who are accustomed to thinking about marketing and sales as "arts" involving great design, compelling messages, creative offers, clever sales plays, and heroic negotiations. I understand that. But it's essential to understand and embrace these admittedly cold, scientific, and highly structured ideas about the revenue process in order to realize the benefits of Revenue Performance Management. That's because for businesses of any reasonable scale and complexity, the revenue process *can* be organized in a structured and repeatable way, and its performance *can* be measured and tuned using analytics and statistics.

That said, there's a reason why manufacturing and quality and supply chain and financial operations were transformed decades ago by these kinds of process-centric approaches, while marketing and sales operations were largely left untouched. Simply put, it's because there *is* a very real art to marketing, and there *is* a very real art to sales. Buyers are people, and people have preferences, quirks, emotions, and unpredictable behaviors. Marketing professionals are people, too, with creative inspiration and strategic vision. And sales professionals are also people, with a highly evolved ability to read other people and find ways of getting deals done.

So while RPM involves the need to adopt structured business processes, formal metrics, and scientific thinking, it must never fail to acknowledge the deep humanity involved as well. RPM may require revenue professionals to learn new skills and adapt to new kinds of formalized methods. But it is not about replacing or devaluing people in the revenue process. To the contrary, it is about laying a rock-solid foundation that channels the creative energies of marketing professionals toward finding and nourishing more prospects. And that, in turn, frees sales professionals to spend more of their time doing what they do best: "getting to yes" with more real buyers.

KEY POINTS

- Implementing RPM requires sales and marketing organizations to adopt new and changed business methods.

- A new generation of thought leaders, consultants, and technology companies has emerged to help companies implement needed changes.

- The initial phase of the revenue process is a form of numbers game—securing the greatest number of potential prospects' names.

- The middle phase involves nourishing and cultivating each prospect, keeping them moving through the stages of their buying process.

- Separating the curious from the serious among potential buyers can make the sales effort much more efficient.

- Structured revenue performance management does not replace the human aspects of marketing and sales; instead, it builds a foundation for their most effective use.

CHAPTER 15

The Nuts and Bolts of a Revenue Cycle Process

I had a fascinating—and, to tell the truth, somewhat scary—experience a few years ago while we were designing our first product at my company, Marketo. My marketing team had organized an amazing series of focus group discussions with some top CMOs and marketing leaders in Silicon Valley. We invited 8 or 10 folks from each group to sit down together and talk about the challenges they faced as marketing leaders. My role was to be a fly on the wall, to listen and learn.

Not surprisingly, the discussion quickly turned to metrics and marketing performance. These marketing leaders knew, as do their counterparts today, that they needed a higher level of accountability for how the money they spend translates into revenue booked by their sales team. But it immediately became clear in watching these focus groups that very few marketing leaders have any sort of formal framework or vocabulary for discussing how to measure, compare over time, or accurately communicate about marketing performance.

The most fascinating part would come when the group started to talk about an almost-iconic topic: "How much should marketing spend to generate a lead?" One CMO would yell out, "$50! If you're spending more than $50 to generate a lead, you're spending too much." Another would reply, "Huh? $50? A lead costs $1,000!" "No, $2,500!" Then another would jump in, "Well, in *my* company, I can generate leads for $16 each." And everyone else would excitedly ask, "Awesome, how do you do that?" These discussions would go on for at least half an hour.

During three different sessions that included this same conversation, not a single participant ever stopped to ask, "Wait a minute! What do we mean by the term 'lead'?" The $16 rock star and the $2,500 laggard never stopped to think that they might be talking about entirely different things—ones that are no more comparable than apples and armadillos.

Some of the marketing leaders in the room were working to create leads for the sale of products costing $1 million or more per deal, while others sold products that could be purchased for $500. So *of course* the cost per lead would be different for these different products and buying scenarios.

Even more interesting was the fact that the marketing leaders were citing cost figures from completely different stages of the buying process. To one, a "lead"[1] meant the name of any person who might vaguely be considered to ever, maybe, someday, *perhaps* buy something. To another, "lead" meant a rigorously qualified buyer, who was known to have a budget, a need, and an active buying process already under way. And it obviously costs more to find and identify a highly qualified buyer than it does to capture a raw and entirely unqualified name, even for identical products and buyers.

Although it was scary to see these discussions play out time and again, I must admit that it wasn't surprising. After all, the marketing demand generation process has historically been characterized by an almost pervasive lack of objective definitions or standardized metrics. This is not only an issue for marketing leaders who are struggling to figure out about how to allocate and invest resources toward creating new leads for their sales colleagues. The lack of definitions and standardization around leads prevents better cooperation between marketing and sales. I have seen literally dozens of companies where the term "lead" is casually bandied about between these two departments, without anyone taking the time to define its meaning. Salespeople think "lead" means a real live one, ready to buy. But the same term could mean a much less qualified prospect to marketing, as my experience

---

[1] I want to acknowledge the confusing use of the term "lead," even in this book. Sometimes the word is used to mean anyone in the entire revenue funnel versus a much more precise meaning of a buyer at a certain specific stage of their process. It's a fact of life that the word gets used in both ways, so always pay attention to which meaning is being used!

with the focus groups confirmed. Marketing would say, "I gave you 50 leads last month." Sales replies, "You did no such thing." And they're both right—within their own private definitions. Mistrust, and all the bad things that come from it, are the inevitable results.

Finally, marketing leaders have no hope of communicating effectively with executive management if they don't have a shared understanding of terms, an agreement as to what metrics actually mean, and a consensus as to which metrics actually *matter* outside of the four walls of the marketing department. Everyone involved with revenue in a company needs a *lingua franca*, a common set of terms with defined meanings. And they need a common agreement as to what is "good" and "bad" relative to any metric.

For revenue professionals, this common language is the Revenue Cycle Model, which we'll now explore in much greater detail.

DEFINING YOUR REVENUE CYCLE MODEL

The first step is to actually define each of the steps or stages of your revenue creation process in rigorous detail. This establishes a common language for consistent measurement and communication across departments (sales, marketing, finance, etc.) and reduces the confusion that occurs when different groups use the same terms differently. Those definitions also form the foundation for a more structured approach to generating new customers. That's because each department now understands its own role and responsibilities in working with potential customers at each stage.

While clarity is of course desirable for its own sake, the ultimate goal here is to bring a company's revenue process to the same level of precision we see in other departments of the corporation. Finance, for example, is effective in most organizations because it follows generally accepted accounting principles that everyone understands and agrees upon. Repeatable, systematic processes are required for business functions to be regarded as professional disciplines. Marketing and sales are no different; they too require a rigorous, quantifiable, and universally understood methodology for finding buyer interest and turning that interest into revenue and cash flow. Additionally, this kind of standardized measurement also allows for internal corporate operating units—and even different companies—to more accurately compare results. The result is to promote a rethinking of the revenue process at every level in the company.

The revenue process should take its cues from the Six Sigma DMAIC approach: *Defining* each stage; *Measuring* key aspects of the process and collecting relevant data metrics; *Analyzing* the data to find exceptions and understand relationships; *Improving* the process continually, including small experiments to help the organization learn; and finally, *Controlling* the process with proper Key Performance Indicators and dashboards so you can identify problems as early as possible.

WALK BEFORE YOU RUN

So, how should your company go about defining its own revenue cycle process? As in almost all endeavors, the best approach is to start simply, then learn and gain experience. Keep looking for ways to improve and evolve your model as your insight grows; don't be afraid to discard aspects that aren't working or to expand areas that provide deeper insights. And of course, results will vary depending on the organization. I have seen very successful RPM adopters end up with very different Revenue Cycle Models. Some, after several years of experience and a sophisticated customer buying process that spans months or even years, might include a dozen or more stages, while others will start with only three or four. Everyone learns to walk before they can run.

But why have stages at all? After all, the buyer, who really controls the process, couldn't care less about your revenue stages. They just want to learn, to be treated right, and decide what they want on their own terms and schedules.

However, there are two key reasons for introducing stages as the foundation of the RPM process. First, they form the basis for measurement; after all, you can't improve a process if you can't measure it. Therefore, you must "take the buyer's temperature" at various points along the continuous buying cycle. These places form the boundaries of each stage, and you give your measurements real meaning and substance by defining them in rigorous terms.

The second reason to divide the buying cycle into stages is to focus on the distinctive phases of the buyer's journey. Buyers have different needs during the exploration and research phase than they do when negotiating for price. By separating the process into steps or stages, even if they are completely arbitrary from the buyer's point of view, you can focus attention on what is most important at that particular point in the process. It helps you to build measurable, testable programs and methods that allow you to excel at each step in the process.

FARMING REVENUE

In Part I, I introduced the oft-used metaphor of the salesperson as "lonely hunter," out to capture dinner. So it seems only fair that I should also introduce a farming metaphor for readers who tend in a more vegetarian direction.

No matter how many steps your unique Revenue Stage Model ultimately grows to include, the revenue process can be separated into three key phases:

1. **Early awareness and preference building, or *Seed Nurturing*.**

    Think of this as planting seeds—that is, initiating small, early stage, not-yet-mature relationships with your customers-to-be. Not every seed you plant will germinate and grow into a mature plant that bears ripe fruit. But the number of seeds you plant, and the nourishment you provide during their early growth, will have everything to do with the ultimate success of your harvest.

    In terms of our revenue model, this is the phase characterized by advertising, brand building, awareness generation, social media interaction, search engine optimization, web page browsing, and the like. Your goal here is to get in front of potential buyers and make them aware of your company and products using compelling messages and incentives. Then, when a buyer is ready to make his or her move, you're there waiting.

2. **Core engagement and relationship development, or *Lead Nurturing*.**

You've planted the seeds, and a good number have sprouted and grown. Now the goal is to nurture the most promising—lavishing water, fertilizer, and attention on the best while thinning and pruning out the weaklings.

This is the phase where you know prospective buyers' names and contact information, and are starting to have some sort of two-way dialog with them. This might be a literal dialog, as in a phone call, or a conceptual dialog—the buyer visits your website, opens an e-mail from you, attends a webinar, and so on. The key during this phase is to support your prospective buyers' need for information, keep your brand and benefits front-of-mind, to monitor and then to measure their level of interest. When one of them "raises their hand"—either explicitly, as by calling your toll free phone number, or implicitly, as by showing a sustained high level of engagement with your website—it's time to move toward the sale.

3. **Qualification to Close.**

It's harvest time; however, realize that not all of your crops will mature at the same rate. You need to identify which fruit is ready for picking at any given moment, and harvest your meal at that instant of perfect ripeness.

In revenue terms, this is the phase where you determine the most likely buyers among all the people or companies with whom you're interacting. You engage them by phone, e-mail, or other channels to qualify them and quantify their true level of interest. Then you focus your sales time and resources on the best. That's when revenue happens.

Figure 15.1 expands upon the typical end-to-end Revenue Cycle Model (the "revenue funnel") that we first saw in Chapter 12. It shows how each of the three phases of the revenue process is made up of several stages along the buyer's journey. This basic model applies to most companies, regardless of size or industry.

Some companies will have fewer stages, some will have many more, and the specific names for the stages will vary. What's more, the revenue stage model will change and evolve as part of the continuous improvement process called for by RPM. Nonetheless, a best-practice revenue cycle will be based on three fundamental principles.

- *Sales resources are relatively expensive.* To provide the highest value, sales should not engage with prospects until those prospects are ready to engage with sales. Sales interactions should start relatively late in the pipeline, once leads have already been well qualified. Companies should use lower-cost channels, usually managed by marketing, to develop relationships with everyone else. In practical terms, this means that marketing owns earlier stages, while the sales team owns later stages. However, in a world where sales and marketing are truly collaborating, departmental ownership should fade into the background in favor of having both teams focus on the activities

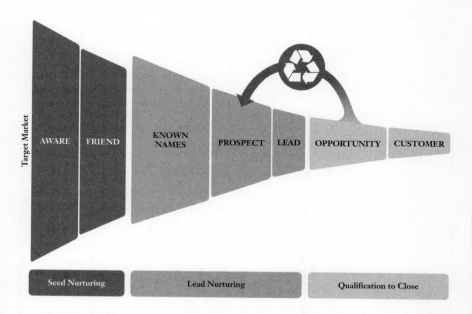

FIGURE 15.1   A Revenue Cycle Model spans three primary stages of the revenue process, and embraces a recycling process where leads flow "backward" from sales to marketing.

that propel buyers through the process as successfully and efficiently as possible.

- *No lead left behind.* Don't let potential customers end up in "lead purgatory." Wherever possible, define "service level agreements" that specify how long a potential customer can sit in a particular stage. That will help to ensure your sales leads either flow forward toward closed revenue, or are returned back to marketing for ongoing nurturing.

- *A prospect's journey from initial awareness to customer is often non-linear.* As discussed in Chapter 12, the revenue cycle is not a linear funnel that flows in only one direction. Sometimes leads originally deemed "sales-ready" are actually not ready for sales. But since you shouldn't let a lead remain stagnant in the system, you want to make sure your revenue cycle has a process for recycling leads as necessary.

Finally, remember that this model is a view of the selling process *through the sellers' eyes.* The prospective buyer doesn't know or care about them. All RPM business practices built around the model must always take this into account.

REVENUE CYCLE STAGES IN DEPTH

For those readers interested in a more in-depth discussion of the Revenue Cycle Model, this sidebar describes each of the steps in our example model, as illustrated in Figure 15.1. It explains the definition of each step, and lists several key business metrics associated with that stage.

SEED NURTURING PHASE

Aware
This first or "top" stage of the Revenue Cycle Model represents that subset of the entire universe of potential customers

in your target market who have become *aware* of your company or products. It doesn't matter what they happen to think about you, or what exposure with your brand created that awareness. Historically, companies used mass media advertising to build awareness—TV, print, radio, outdoor, sponsorship, and public relations. These days, they also use highly targeted online and offline programs as well as social media to help the right buyers learn about the company.

Metrics

- Brand recognition—aided and unaided

- Share of voice

- Reach

- Mentions

- Aggregate website traffic

Friend

Friends not only know your brands and products; they have positive associations and preferences for them. Those preferences reflect the aggregate of all the interactions that the potential customer has had, either directly or indirectly, concerning your company. You can occasionally create this brand preference, which we'll refer to using the social media idiom "like," with advertising. However, "liking" comes about much more frequently when buyers encounter great content and thought leadership and engage with brand advocates in traditional or social channels.

That's why it can be so valuable to build a company's social following. For example, a potential customer who "Likes" a brand on Facebook is opting to receive updates and learn more about that company. When the brand can *create* positive interactions with a prospect before that person is actually in the market to buy, that individual is much more likely to select a company

(continued)

(*continued*)

they already like whenever they're finally ready to make their purchase.

Metrics

- Brand preference

- Social followers/friends

- Engagement (comments, likes, etc.)

- Message multiplication/"reverberation" (retweets, shares, links, etc.)

LEAD NURTURING PHASE

Names

This stage begins when the company first collects an individual's contact information to store in their marketing database. We purposely called this stage "Names" to distinguish between people we know how to contact but otherwise don't know much about, and those we would regard as "Leads" because they are showing real buying behavior. Just because someone throws a business card into a fishbowl to win an iPad, attends an event you sponsor, or is on an account executive's target list doesn't mean they are qualified or ready to buy your product. In fact, they may not even know who you are. That's why the "Names" group can sometimes be even broader than "Aware."

Metrics

- Number of new names generated per month, quarter, and so on, by source.

- Quarter-over-quarter/year-over-year database growth by business unit, lead type, and so on.

- Invest per new name by lead type and source.

- Average age of names in the database.

Prospect

This stage refers to individuals who are qualified and engaged with your company, but not yet ready to connect with your sales staff. They have had a meaningful interaction with your brand, and are aware they are in your database and have opted in to future interactions.

Metrics

- Number of qualified prospects, by type.

- Conversion rate from all names to qualified prospects.

- Time to convert names to prospects.

- Average age of prospect inventory.

Lead

A "Lead," as we use the term here, is a marketing-qualified buyer who is ready to engage with Sales. While the exact definition of a "lead" should be left up to the organization's sales and marketing teams, it should include a behavioral component to show that the potential buyer is significantly engaged or seems ready to buy.

Metrics

- Number of leads by business, type, and so on.

- Conversion rate from prospect to lead.

- Number of "fast leads" who came in hot, versus "slow leads" who needed nurturing.

- Adherence with lead follow-up Service Level Agreements such as speed of first contact, time to disposition, number of untouched and "stale" leads.

- Outcome/disposition of leads.

(continued)

(*continued*)

QUALIFICATION TO CLOSE PHASE

Opportunity

The Opportunity stage refers to potential customers who are qualified and known to sales, and are actively engaged with a sales representative. Significantly, this opportunity stage is the customary start of the traditional sales cycle at most companies. It is often further subdivided into a number of smaller sales sub-stages within a company's SFA or CRM system.

Metrics

- Number of opportunities.

- Number of marketing-sourced opportunities.

- Conversion rate from lead to opportunity.

- Average opportunity value.

Customer

The Customer stage is the culmination of the funnel sales cycle process. It represents new business that actually results from those who were previously at the opportunity stage. However, it doesn't conclude the relationship. In fact, at many companies, the customer stage becomes the beginning of a new revenue cycle for cross-sell, upsell, and retention.

Metrics

- Conversion rate from opportunity to customer.

- Average deal size.

- Total number of customers.

- Number of new and repeat customers.

This chapter has provided a framework for defining, communicating, and measuring a complete revenue process. However, building a framework is comparatively easy. The hard work is actually *creating revenue*: allocating investments, building marketing programs, measuring buyer engagement, maximizing sales effectiveness, and continuously improving all of them to drive outsize revenue growth. Each of the next three chapters will explore the business process that takes place within the three phases of the Revenue Cycle Model, and explain how you can design, build, measure, and improve each over time.

KEY POINTS

- Marketing professionals often attach very different meanings to the same terms and metrics, making collaboration and communication difficult within the marketing team as well as with other groups in the company.

- The Revenue Cycle Model provides the basis for a common vocabulary describing stages in the sales-marketing process.

- Clear definitions help to clarify departmental roles, responsibilities, processes, and performance indicators.

- A company's revenue model can start out simply, but will evolve, improve, and become more refined over time.

- A staged model of the revenue process helps the seller focus more effectively on each distinctive phase of the buyer's journey.

- Three key stages of the revenue model are: early seed nurturing, engaged lead nurturing, and closing on those ready for harvesting.

- Key principles behind the revenue model are that sales is an expensive resource; that leads should never be left behind; and that buyers' journeys are often nonlinear.

CHAPTER 16

"Seed Nurturing"—Helping Your Buyers Find You

The awareness that the buyer is in control means that you must change the way you think about finding prospective buyers. A marketing demand generation professional's job is no longer to *find* buyers; it is to help buyers *find you*. And since you never know when any individual buyer is going to be looking for you or considering a purchase, your task is to build a pervasive and easy-to-find presence across multiple digital and traditional channels. This way, your brand and product information are easily accessible the moment the prospective buyer begins to look.

Not so long ago, information about your company and its offerings was not readily available, online or offline. Beyond reading an advertisement, analyst review, or printed catalog, the only way a buyer could learn more about your products or services was to meet with a sales representative. As a result, prospective buyers were willing to talk to a salesperson early in their evaluation and research process, well before getting serious about buying anything. For the sales team, it was a necessary evil to spend time with such early stage buyers.

As we saw in Chapter 4, the traditional marketing demand generation approaches that evolved during this era grew up with a hunting mentality. Tactics such as telemarketing, direct mail, trade shows, and other forms of mass advertising evolved to help marketers find buyers and push their messages on to them. However, all these tactics shared a common trait: they were only effective if they interrupted whatever else the buyer was doing in order to attract their attention.

The problem is that today's customers don't *want* to be interrupted. In fact, they don't want to feel like they are being "marketed to" at all. And they are increasingly using their control to screen out, throw out, and tune out your unwanted marketing messages using DVRs, spam filters, caller ID, and so on.

Some marketers responded by dialing up the volume and intensity of their traditional communications. But if you really believe that the buyer is in control, then the solution to attention scarcity is not to be louder; it's to be different and compelling to the buyer's interests.

Fortunately, there are points during every buying cycle when the customer is actively seeking information. According to the Pew Research Center's Internet & American Life Project, 78 percent of Internet users today conduct product research online. And in October 2010, think tank SRI International found that 46 percent of web searches are for information about products and services. From typing something into Google to initiate research, to putting together a short list, to building an ROI justification, buyers want trusted information to help them. And they are seeking that information by searching online and asking their social networks. Therefore, the company that best provides them the information they are seeking, at the moment they are looking, is in the best position to earn their eventual business.

That's why today's revenue-focused marketing professionals need to be experts in what has come to be called "inbound marketing" or, in keeping with our farming metaphor, "seed nurturing." Inbound marketing is the process of helping prospective customers to find your company, often before they are actively looking to make a purchase, and then progressively turning that early awareness into brand preference, knowledge of your products and services, and a buyer's journey that ultimately leads to booked revenue for your business.

The central tenets of inbound marketing are to create great and compelling content, to use that content as bait to attract, educate, and win potential buyers' interest—what we've called "awareness." You then want to get that bait in front of the buyer in a pervasive way by promoting it online and across social networks by mastering such techniques as search engine optimization (SEO) and viral marketing campaigns.

To do this well, marketers must think differently. It's not about having the best tagline or most exciting creative materials (although there is always a place for branding, as we'll see in Chapter 21). Marketers have to think like a publisher who is tasked with creating consistent, relevant content for every stage of the revenue cycle. When it's done right, this approach produces dramatically better results than traditional marketing techniques that rely on interrupting the customer.

Well-known speaker and author on the topic of web marketing David Meerman Scott puts it this way: "Prior to the web, organizations had only two significant choices to attract attention: buy expensive advertising or get third-party ink from the media. But the web has changed the rules." Instead of renting buyer attention from third parties, which is exactly what interruption-based advertising is all about, seed nurturing means creating your own audience and attracting your own attention. Brains are important here—not budget.

ATTRACTING BUYERS ACROSS THE REVENUE CYCLE WITH CONTENT MARKETING

Publishing great content is at the heart of finding new buyers in today's economy. Content can be anything your organization creates and shares to tell its story—your website, blog, podcasts, videos, tweets, whitepapers, e-books, photos, presentations, LinkedIn advertisements, webinars, press releases, ROI calculators, brochures, workbooks, and so on.

Regardless of the form that content takes, it will need to account for the fact that potential customers are in different stages of the revenue cycle. Some buyers already know what solution they're seeking, while others don't even know they have a problem. You can attract the former by providing information that helps them evaluate possibilities and recognize issues they wouldn't see on their own. This kind of content often includes buying guides, checklists, analyst reports, webinars, and even in-person events. This will show buyers that your company understands how to solve their problems.

However, the buyers who don't yet know they have a need aren't actively searching for solutions. Fortunately, these individuals still consume information online; they're just attracted by different types of content. Some of the things that work best here are research data, engaging videos, curated lists, infographics, as well as highly relevant and useful thought leadership and expertise. Content for this early stage audience will usually be short-form and consumable in just a minute or two, often on a mobile device. Just remember, a buyer who looks at this content is not likely to make an immediate purchase. But by connecting with them before they are even looking for a solution— while their anti-marketing shields are down—you make it more likely that they will think of your company as a trusted advisor and thought leader when they are eventually ready to make a purchase. The boss in *Glengarry Glen Ross* got it wrong; success with content marketing is not about "always be closing"—it's "always be helping."

Ultimately, this means that marketing must invest a significant level of resources in creating and disseminating content. This content creation process goes well beyond the traditional tasks of building product collateral—data sheets or tear sheets—and even beyond the newer tradition of maintaining an extensive website. You must also deliver it to online and offline channels; web and social channels; video, text, audio presentations, and more. It's also critical to reuse content, since one set of key ideas and meaty information can often be transformed into a series of tweets, webinar slides, a web microsite, or grist for any number of other media. Companies that have fully embraced Revenue Performance Management have content marketing functions that act as a key locus of attention and investment within their overall revenue organization.

HELP YOUR CONTENT GET FOUND WITH OPTIMIZATION AND PROMOTION

However, even the best content in the world won't drive revenue if nobody sees it. This is where search engine marketing becomes critical. Your buyers are searching on Google, Bing, and industry-specific buying sites, so you need to make sure your content shows up when they do. And as buyers spend more and more time on social networks including Facebook, LinkedIn, and Twitter, social media marketing becomes an important way to promote content as well.

There are two basic forms of search engine marketing. The first, search engine optimization (SEO), is about achieving high rankings in the *organic* listings that show up in the center of a search engine's results page. Clicks on these links are free, but it's entirely up to the search engine's algorithm to decide what goes on top. The second, pay-per-click advertising (PPC) or search engine marketing (SEM), is how the search engines make money. Companies bid for rank positioning among the ads that show up on the very top and right of the results page, and they pay a fee every time someone clicks on their ad.

SEO is especially important. According to recent research from GroupM, a whopping 92 percent of clicks from a search engine go to the free, organic listings. A separate Optify study found that 58 percent of all those clicks go to the first three sites listed. So how can you ensure your content achieves top organic rankings? There is an entire industry devoted to decoding how search engines like Google rank results, but a few basic principles stand out. First, content must be relevant and specific to the search you want to rank for. If you want to rank for the search "industrial ball bearings," then you must have a web page that's all about industrial ball bearings.

However, the content on the page makes up only about 25 percent of the search engine's decision about what to rank. The other 75 percent is made up of what are called "off-page" factors, the most important being the number and type of outside links that point to your web pages. To put it simply, Google counts each link to the page as a vote for that page. Links from pages which themselves have more votes are worth more. Perhaps the most important piece of advice is: The more distinctive and truly compelling your content, the more people will link to it.

Social media platforms are increasingly important for helping buyers find your content for two reasons. First, companies can use social media as a way to promote their content directly by building their lists of friends and followers. From there, the best content can "go viral" as buyers and influencers share it and reshare it with each other socially. These are increasingly becoming critical parts of companies' online strategy. According to a recent study from advertising firms Starcom MediaVest Group and Rubinson Partners, social sharing now produces an estimated 10 percent of all traffic to corporate

FIGURE 16.1 **Effective use of organic search engine optimization (SEO) and pay-per-click advertising, also known as search engine marketing (SEM) is essential to seed nurturing.**

websites, although search still counts for at least twice as much. The second reason is that social media are increasingly important as a signal to search engines' ranking algorithms. Just like links, each social share is considered a vote for a particular site, and shares from people who have more authority (e.g., followers) are worth even more than casual visitors.

There are other ways to promote content as well: blogging, issuing press releases, proactively reaching out to influencers such as bloggers, news organizations, analysts, and others to let them know about your content online, and "advertising" it on your company's website or elsewhere on the web. Finally, there is a role for traditional outbound marketing techniques in a full content promotion strategy. Demand marketing professionals can use e-mail, paid promotions such as content syndication, banner advertising, e-mail sponsorships, print advertising, outdoor advertising, and third-party events to distribute content to new audiences as well.

TRANSFORMING AWARENESS INTO PREFERENCE

So now you've created amazing content and lots of potential buyers know about your company. Your website is getting tons of traffic, and people are talking about your company on social media sites. You have awareness, and the first stage of your Revenue Cycle Model captures and measures how effectively you are extending your reach to new potential buyers over time. The next step is to transfer that awareness to preference. It doesn't do you any good to make a lot of people aware of your company and products if they develop a negative impression of you along the way; that's not how you get them to buy.

The best early-stage content follows two key rules to create a positive and impactful impression. First, it must be *relevant* to the buyer. Generic materials will not result in positive preference. Second, your content must be *helpful*, not promotional. Early stage buyers are keenly aware of content that seems to simply promote your company. You're not supposed to be telling the buyer what *you* want them to know; you're helping them find and learn what *they* want to know. So make sure you always put your audience's interests before your own before creating any piece of content. Anything that seems too promotional will prompt prospects to break off their relationship with you forever by literally opting out or, more likely, emotionally opting out by just not paying attention.

However, you need more than high quality content to establish a positive vibe with prospective buyers. Potential customers will also look to other sources—friends, consultants, bloggers, professional analysts, published reviews, and a myriad others—in order to decide what they think about your company and products. These sources are called *influencers*, and they are critical to any modern revenue creation plan. And with the emergence of social media, where a collective opinion can form quickly and be immediately accessible to anyone who is looking, the role of influencers is increasing every day.

As a result, content marketing must be paired hand-in-glove with effective influencer marketing. This requires an explicit and well-executed program to identify key influencers by name—bloggers, journalists, analysts, and social media thought leaders, to name a few—and to communicate with those constituencies in concert with your content marketing efforts directed to end buyers. Influencers often look for an extra flow of information, an inside track to your product plans, pricing, strategies, and so on. That puts them in a better position to form their own opinions, and guide buyers to "like" you.

If you looked at a typical organization chart for a marketing department today, you would likely find that the people responsible for "influencer relations" report quite a distance away from the people who are responsible for demand marketing. In most marketing organizations, the people who communicate with influencers are part of the "PR team," or marketing communications department. Their colleagues responsible for building leads report into a completely different place in the organization. In Chapter 25, we will look at the organization chart implications of adopting a Revenue Performance Management strategy. But let it suffice to say at this point that marketing team members responsible for communicating with influencers need to move much closer to their content marketing colleagues who are responsible for communicating with prospective buyers.

CONVERTING PREFERENCE INTO LEADS

Okay, your buyers have consulted with their friends and other wise advisors across online and offline channels and their interest is piqued. They have learned something, and formed a good impression. They like you, and are open to buying from you.

Yet the prospective buyer is likely still anonymous to you at this sensitive stage of the revenue funnel. That is, while the buyer may know you, you don't know the buyer. The next step is to gain permission to extend the conversation into more interactive and intimate channels by having the buyer provide you with his or her contact information.

Consider an analogy: Perhaps you went out with your friends for a night on the town, maybe to meet someone (the buyer who knows what he wants), or maybe just to have fun (the buyer who doesn't know she has a need). Either way, across the room, there he or she is. You make eye contact. Share a smile. Have a brief chat, maybe a drink or a dance. As "last call" is announced, you ask and he or she agrees to give you a phone number (for texting, of course). You've turned an anonymous interaction into a known relationship, one you can build into something more substantial over time.

The revenue cycle process is quite similar. At some point, you will have built enough trust with potential buyers to ask them to provide their contact information. Often, this is in exchange for something of value, perhaps an invitation to a webinar or access to a high-quality whitepaper. Of course, be sure not to ask for the contact information too soon in the relationship! Just as you wouldn't ask a potential date for his or her phone number at the moment you first meet, you don't want to always require buyers to fill out a form to see your early stage content. Rather, you want that content to be seen by as many people as possible, perhaps even go viral. But at the right time, capturing an e-mail address and/or phone number is essential to deepening the relationship and moving the potential buyer further down the revenue cycle.

Of course, your company probably acquires prospects' names through other means as well, including trade shows; referrals from customers, partners, and employees; sales relationships; and networking. Regardless of the source, don't expect your new prospects to turn into qualified leads right away. Just as a first date isn't ready for a marriage proposal, a prospect who registers to receive a whitepaper or who visits your booth at a tradeshow is likely not yet ready and willing to engage with a sales representative.

Remember this: If you think of someone who just gave you their name and e-mail address as a "lead" and hand that name over to a salesperson, you will have dug a deeper hole in the dysfunction between marketing and sales. You have a *name*, not a lead; it's not time for the marketing team to declare "mission accomplished." Instead, you need to deepen the relationship over time by interacting in a variety of settings, learning more about each other's needs and capabilities while progressing seamlessly from one interaction to the next. And you need to know when to commit more resources to the relationship as well as when to pull back and give the prospect some space.

This "dating" process is called lead nurturing. It is defined as the process of building a relationship with qualified prospects that are not yet sales-ready. Similarly, the process of identifying when the prospect is actually ready for sales is known as lead scoring. We'll cover both in more detail in the next chapter.

KEY POINTS

- Building a pervasive presence across multiple channels is essential for prospective buyers to find you.

- Consistently having the most interesting, relevant, and helpful content is critical to attracting favorable attention from potential buyers.

- Astute use of search engines as marketing tools is essential for inbound marketing—that is, helping early-stage buyers find out about you.

- Starting a relationship with a potential buyer is a lot like starting a new relationship in your personal life. It takes time, and sensitivity to taking the right actions at an appropriate time.

CHAPTER 17

The Art and Science of Nurturing and Scoring Leads

The more successful that you are at casting a wide net with a seed nurturing process—that is, using web tools, quality content, and inbound marketing to meet prospective buyers—the more likely you are to capture names and begin marketing relationships with people at increasingly earlier stages in their buying process. At the same time, however, self-directed and empowered buyers want to conduct the process on their own terms. So they resist engaging with sales until they're largely done with their research. In some cases, buyers can be as much as 80 percent of the way to making up their minds by the time they're willing to talk with a salesperson.

This has led to a massive gap between the time when the name of an early stage buyer is captured by a vendor, and the time when that buyer can be considered a true sales lead. In fact, according to a survey by revenue resource site RainToday, fewer than 25 percent of the new buyer names that vendors capture are actually ready to engage with sales when they first enter a marketing database. Of course, some of the others will never qualify, but as many as 70 percent of the total *will* eventually buy a product from you—or from your competitors.

Successful inbound marketing will capture more names, especially more early-stage names. However, it'll also gather people who *don't* want to talk to your sales team. This has all the ingredients for turning a genuine success into a real disaster. If you toss those leads over the wall to sales before they're ready, you're just feeding the sales department's long-standing complaint about the quality of marketing leads. Even worse, you risk annoying or even alienating the prospect who doesn't yet want to talk to a salesperson. Salespeople excel at *closing* business, not developing it. So early stage leads in their hands often end up in limbo and get dropped on the floor, which in turn means that companies end up ignoring anywhere from 20 to 35 percent of their potential future revenue. And to add insult to injury, they're wasting the resources they have already spent on finding these new buyers in the first place.

So what should you do with the surfeit of early stage leads that seed nurturing helps you create?

The answer is to implement a critical new revenue process called *lead nurturing*—the process of building and maintaining relationships with qualified prospects regardless of their timing to buy. Prospects may not want to be sold to, but they welcome help and support with their own learning and research process. And buyers do want to build growing connections with the vendors they are considering. Ultimately, the goal of lead nurturing is to connect prospects with salespeople at the moment each prospect is ready to buy, whenever that might be.

In addition to building relationships with prospective buyers, lead nurturing is all about treating prospects as valuable business assets that companies must track and account for, as they would with capital equipment or finished goods inventory. Gone are the days where leads get dropped on the floor, sit in perpetual limbo, or just vanish into thin air. Of course, some leads will still go away, because people change jobs, or buy from a competitor, or simply because they opt out of your lead nurturing process. But since lead nurturing accounts for these individuals as they go away, it enables a far more sophisticated closed-loop business analysis and optimization of the revenue process.

Once you embrace the discipline of keeping all new leads within marketing (instead of immediately sending them to sales) and nurturing them until "the moment they are ready to buy," you immediately face these questions: How do I know *when* they are ready to buy? Which leads do you send to sales? When? And why? This is where a companion revenue process comes in: *lead scoring*.

Lead scoring is the systematic process of monitoring, evaluating, and assigning scores to buyer behavior in order to measure their activity, interest, engagement, and urgency of action. Monitored behaviors include things like web page visits, tweets, link clicks on your website, answering a phone call, watching a video, or myriad other actions that have meaning in the context of a buying cycle. This process allows you to develop a ranked list of how good each lead is, based on business rules that marketing and sales teams create jointly. This ranking determines when a lead gets passed from the marketing-driven nurturing process over to sales for the pursuit of a deal. It is designed to help salespeople prioritize their time and allocate more to those prospects most likely to actually buy.

Both lead nurturing and lead scoring are critically important business processes. They form the foundation for a successful Revenue Performance Management strategy. So let's explore each of them in a bit more detail.

BUILDING ENGAGEMENT AND DEVELOPING RELATIONSHIPS WITH LEAD NURTURING

Virtually every business will have some prospective buyers who follow a fast and direct path from the start to the finish of their buying cycle. They almost drop out of the sky, with a clearly identified need, money in their pockets, and their minds made up by the moment they first give you their contact information. For them, marketing has already done its job. These are leads that should be in a salesperson's hands right away, and there's no need to slow them down with over-communication. But these "fast movers" probably represent just a few percent of all the names you capture in your wide net through inbound marketing and other early-stage customer acquisition efforts.

Lead nurturing is about staying in touch with everyone else— those buyers who have opted to give you their names and contact information, but have neither made up their minds, secured a budget, nor done enough research to decide whether they're actually in the market at all.

What lead nurturing is *not* about is sending out a generic e-newsletter on a semi-regular basis, randomly calling leads every few weeks to see if they're ready to buy, blasting your entire database with new case studies, or pushing content that promotes your products and services but is irrelevant to your prospects' interests or needs at their particular stage of buying. Instead, lead nurturing is just like building any long-term relationship—perhaps the one that started unexpectedly during the night on the town we mentioned in Chapter 16. You need to be a good partner, foster respect and trust, be a good listener, and keep things interesting. You need to be consistent and relevant.

So what does a disciplined lead nurturing process look like? At the highest level, there are first-impression campaigns, stay-in-touch campaigns, and campaigns that attempt to motivate or accelerate buying. Here are some ideas about each:

1. **Make a Great First Impression.**

   Just as with our personal lives, starting a long-term lead nurturing relationship with a prospect begins by making a positive first impression. What you say and do, and how you act when you first meet someone, affects how they perceive you for the rest of time. So what should you be doing to lay the right foundation from the beginning? Without doubt, the first order of business is to make sure you have obtained permission (i.e., an "opt in") from the prospect to send ongoing communications to him or her. Even better, you should allow prospects to customize their preferences for the types and frequency of those communications.

   As we discussed in Chapter 16, think carefully about how your content matches up with where each prospect is in his or her buying cycle. Content like thought leadership, research data, and videos tends to be appropriate for early stage buyers. A good way to tell if a piece of content will work for an early stage buyer is to ask yourself if the information you're providing would be interesting or useful to them even if they never end up buying from you. If the answer is yes, then it's probably good early-stage content.

2. **Y'all Stay In Touch Now.**

   Once you've established a positive initial relationship with a prospect, your goal is to stay top-of-mind with him or her over time. This typically means having a relevant interaction with them every two or three weeks, often over e-mail or the phone, although some companies also use other channels such as SMS (text messages), social media, and video. The key to success here is to maintain a flow of relevant and engaging content; if it's not relevant, then the prospect is likely to tune out or opt out.

The goals of staying in touch are twofold: First, it is simply to keep your brand and your key messages front-of-mind for your buyer. It's a noisy world out there with lots of people loudly clamoring for attention. Even if a prospect started out with a great first impression of your company and its products, it's way too easy for them to forget about you. Secondly, these consistent communications are essential to ascertaining buyer intent. You'll remain aware and can react quickly and assertively if a buyer starts to move toward a purchase process.

Consider this example: You've been in touch with a prospective buyer for a year and have been sending out a high-quality thought leadership e-mail every month, tailored to his interests. However, for months the prospect hasn't opened your e-mail or clicked on any of its links to follow-up information. Then all of a sudden, for two months in a row, the prospect is all over your e-mails—clicking on them, forwarding them, or sharing them in a social context. It's not guaranteed, but there's likely a buying sign there. It's time to make your move and send this lead to sales.

During this stay-in-touch phase, content such as analyst reports, buying guides, request for proposal (RFP) templates, and return on investment (ROI) calculators can work best, particularly for B2B industries. Finally, as prospects show increased buying signals, they typically value hard information like feature/function details, prices, reputation information, competitive comparisons, and so on.

3. **Have I Got an Offer for You!**

Motivation campaigns, which attempt to break buyers out of a box of complacency, may be appropriate from time-to-time. The point of these is to nudge a buyer into action, perhaps with a special offer, or some other incentive to "act now!" As in all relationship building, these nudges shouldn't be random. The right time for a motivation campaign usually comes when a prospect has taken a specific action or shown a specific behavior. Alternatively, a prospect who has not inter- acted in a meaningful way within a certain time period (say, six months) could receive a special high-value offer to recapture their attention and reignite their interest.

Keep in mind that regardless of the type of campaign, lead nur- turing is ultimately about a two-way dialog between buyer and seller, one conducted over time and across a variety of channels. As in any real-world conversation, it requires you to listen and adapt.

Imagine if you were invited to a great party, and decided that you needed to prepare for some conversation by scripting a few interesting topics about sports and wine. You might feel well prepared as you wade into the room. But if the first person you meet couldn't care less about sports and doesn't drink, it would be a huge mistake to stick to your script. You'd be considered boring, if not outright obnoxious. So while you might want to have a few starter ideas for conversations, it's also essential to listen to your conversation partners and respond to where they want to take things. If they want to talk about food, maybe you can find some common ground.

You can't plan a real-world lead nurturing "conversation" in advance any more than you can script the conversations you have at a party. Instead, nurturing campaigns must listen and react to each buy- er's behaviors and signals. Effective lead nurturing processes have to discern the type of content that prospects request—which e-mails they open and click, how often they visit your website, what pages they visit when they're there, what they say on social networks, which phone calls get returned, and so on—and then adjust accordingly.

Finally, it's crucial to note that lead nurturing is about communi- cating one-to-one with individual people. But in many B2B sales situa- tions, there's a team involved in evaluating and purchasing products or services. In fact, according to marketing research firm MarketingSherpa, even small companies (those with 100 to 500 employees) have an aver- age of seven people involved in a buying decision; that number can go as high as 21 individuals on a buying committee at larger companies.

Effective nurturing content needs to speak to each of them and address their unique needs. Key analytics associated with team-oriented nurturing will identify signs that your initial contacts are spreading the word across the organization.

IDENTIFYING THE HOTTEST LEADS AND OPPORTUNITIES WITH LEAD SCORING

While a good conversation is always gratifying, the point of lead nurturing is not simply to have meaningful conversations with your prospects. This process is aimed to tee up revenue, guide prospects through their self-directed research and evaluation cycles, and keep them warm until their budget and need and timing are right for a sales cycle to start.

However, lead nurturing is not about automated selling. While it's true that in some businesses the end point of effective lead nurturing is a self-service store purchase or an e-commerce transaction, for many others the sales art is required to convert buyer interest into booked revenue.

An issue immediately arises as companies master content-driven inbound marketing for lead acquisition. If your content is good and your marketing techniques are effective, a *lot* of people will take the bait. They'll give you their names and contact information in exchange for your content, and thus enter into your lead nurturing process. In some cases, the number of people entering into the early stage of lead nurturing can be 10 or even a hundred times as large as the number of actual buyers in that group. Moreover, among those people who will buy *someday*, there are a few who will move very quickly; others will take much longer. Finally, some will be engaged in active buying; they've already made a personal or corporate decision to buy and they're just choosing among vendors or otherwise completing a formal procurement process. There are others, whom I call latent buyers, who are potentially intrigued by what you have to offer, but have not made any explicit decision to buy.

You therefore need a way to separate the wheat from the chaff; to sort the fast movers from the slowpokes; and to differentiate between those prospects who are leaning forward toward buying, and others who may represent real opportunity but need more time and energy to get to "yes." *Lead scoring* is how you do all these things.

Keep in mind as well that none of these attributes—wheat/chaff, fast/slow, active/latent—are binary. All across your revenue funnel, prospects will fall into every shade of gray along these dimensions. So lead scoring isn't about trying to figure out which prospects are "good" and which are "bad"; instead it's about evaluating and ranking the likelihood that each prospect will buy. You continuously determine which leads should flow to sales based on their rankings, and which will continue to be nurtured in marketing's capable hands.

Lead scoring can substantially improve sales effectiveness by helping salespeople to focus on the most promising opportunities. According to a 2009 report by sales consultancy CSO Insights, companies that say it's easy to get information about prioritizing sales efforts achieve an average of 97 percent of their revenue plan, while companies that say it's hard achieve an average of only 79 percent. When your sales team spends more of its time selling to the right people—those actually *most likely to buy*—they achieve higher win rates, shorter sales cycles, faster sales ramp times, and higher overall revenue productivity.

Because lead scoring is the process that determines which leads go to sales and which ones don't, it must be jointly owned and tended by marketing and sales. This means that both groups must get down to the nitty-gritty definitions of what a lead, a good lead, and a great lead are. They need to determine which attributes of behavior (for example, frequent buyer engagement with product and pricing information as distinct from those who only engage with high-level thought leadership material) and profile (for example, demographic and company-specific information like job title, industry, company size, etc.) suggest who are the most likely buyers to actually complete a sales transaction.

In a world where marketing is from Venus and sales is from Mars, compounded by a legacy of distrust from both sides around lead quality and quantity, establishing a joint lead scoring profile can be a challenge. But it can also be just the ticket to breaking the ice and propelling both marketing and sales toward a far more collaborative relationship.

At the start, lead scoring can be very simple: You pick a small number of objective buyer behaviors and a few buyer profile elements, and give them a grade to indicate their buying readiness. But instead of a letter grade like A, B, or C, a lead scoring process typically assigns numerical points for different scores, so that the scores for different attributes can be added together. You can then use these objective criteria to rank all the leads participating in your nurturing process, and filter the best ones—those who bubble to the top—to hand off to sales. Because the criteria are objective and defined in simple terms that everyone can understand, they offer a great way to build trust and common ground between marketing and sales.

A SIMPLE LEAD SCORING EXAMPLE

The following simple example gives a bit more detail about how lead scoring might work in practice. Consider, for example, a manufacturer of enterprise security firewalls we'll call SecureCo. SecureCo's products are typically purchased by technical security specialists in the IT departments of large companies. Their inbound marketing features lots of great thought leadership content to educate executives, line of business managers, IT professionals, and others about the nature of current Internet security threats. As a result, their seed nurturing efforts attract many interested, but unqualified buyers, into the top of their revenue funnel. Their challenge is how to get the most qualified, or real buyers, into the hands of sales.

This company might create a three-attribute lead scoring process to sort out the best buyers.

1. Job Title

   Executives and business managers are interested in SecureCo's web pages that contain authoritative information describing modern security threats. But in practice, SecureCo sells sophisticated technical products, so most of its

   (continued)

(continued)

buyers come out of the technical ranks of IT organizations. But since executives are very influential in purchases, they can't be ignored. So SecureCo's marketing and sales team might agree to score prospects based on job title, and assign 30 points to someone with an IT technical job title, like "IT Security Specialist." They might assign 20 points to senior executive titles, like CIO or CFO, and maybe 10 points to other titles, since there can be many diverse influencers in their buying cycles.

2. Company Size

SecureCo's products are designed to meet the needs of large corporations, but the kinds of security threats they address apply to companies of all sizes. As a result, their thought leadership content attracts potential buyers from companies of all sizes. However, prospects from small companies rarely buy SecureCo's products; they're simply too sophisticated for small companies. So SecureCo might assign 30 points to prospects from companies with 2,000 or more employees; 20 points to prospects from companies with 500–2,000 employees; and 0 points to prospects from smaller companies.

3. Website Engagement

SecureCo has a fantastic website, divided into content sections designed to appeal to different web visitors. Some pages speak to executives about security threats and why a product like SecureCo's is needed; others dive into nitty-gritty detail about different product models and features. It seems pretty clear to SecureCo's marketing and sales leaders that almost no one except a qualified buyer would spend any time looking at the most technical pages on their website.

As a result, SecureCo assigns 50 points to prospects who visited the detailed product pages on their company's website within the past week. They assign 20 points to prospects who visited within the past two months, but not last week, and 10 points to prospects who visited their technical product pages at some point, but not within the past two months. Others who never visited the product pages get zero points.

With this simple scoring model, SecureCo can make a pretty good guess about how qualified and ready any given lead might be. Tim, an IT technician from a big company who was just on their website this week, gets $30 + 30 + 50 = 110$ points. Rajiv, a CIO from a big company who checked out their website six weeks ago, gets $30 + 20 + 20 = 70$ points. Suzanne, an IT technician from a small company who was just on the product pages, gets $30 + 0 + 50 = 80$ points. And Daniel, an IT technician from a big company who hasn't been on SecureCo's website for six months, gets $30 + 30 + 10 = 70$ points. A college student working on a research paper might get $0 + 0 + 0 = 0$ points.

It's easy to see how this lead scoring model percolates the most qualified prospects to the top of the heap. In order to achieve greater sales efficiency and revenue performance, SecureCo chooses to spend their sales staff's valuable time primarily on highly qualified prospects. So they set a lead scoring threshold of 90 points. Prospects with fewer than 90 points stay within the nurturing process; those over the threshold are passed to sales. So in the example above, Tim would be passed to sales.

Note too that this is a dynamic process, not a one-time scoring calculation. If Daniel, the otherwise qualified IT professional, returned to SecureCo's product pages after a six-month absence, his score would be immediately recalculated, from its previous value of 70 to a new value of $30 + 30 + 50 = 110$. This would be a signal, or trigger, to move Daniel immediately from the nurturing process into sales. You got a bite and have a live one on the line!

How do you come up with these criteria and scores? It's a judgment call at first. Marketing and sales leaders, as well as front-line revenue professionals, usually have a pretty good intuitive idea of what describes a likely buyer. You can always refine your lead nurturing and scoring system over time, so the goal in getting started is to establish a basic framework. Once lead nurturing and lead scoring processes are up and running, you can use analytics to augment human judgment, drive continuous refinement, and increase precision in your ability to identify the most likely buyers.

As in the case of lead nurturing, you'll first apply lead scoring at the individual level. However, it also applies to entire buying teams in businesses where that makes sense. In this case, the process is called "account scoring," and the grades assigned to buyers are aggregated across a number of individuals. But things can get complicated here very fast, since aggregating scores for a team is not as simple as adding them all together. For example, there's no reason to think that a team of 20 people would be more likely to buy than a team of 10 people; but if you added up their scores in a naïve way, they'd likely have a much higher score. So the design of algorithms for accurate scoring of buying teams is at the forefront of current research into Revenue Performance Management.

PASSING THE BATON FROM MARKETING TO SALES

When marketing and sales teams agree upon and establish a lead scoring model, a company using Revenue Performance Management methodologies is ready to continuously rank its leads and define when a prospective buyer should be moved forward into a sales campaign. But first, let me emphasize the significance of *continuously* scoring and ranking leads. Lead scoring is not something you do once, or even once a month. It is a continuous process. Buyers' scores could change every time they take action—say, visiting a web page or attending a webinar. That's how you are able to respond instantly to signals from your prospects, and get the hottest prospects in touch with sales right now. And you need a software system to implement that kind of process on a corporate scale, which is the topic of Chapter 20.

Continuously ranking lead scores makes it much easier to determine which leads to pass on to sales: the best ones. Depending on the level of your sales staffing and capacity relative to the size of your revenue pipeline, that might be the best 1 percent, the best 5 percent, or even the best 50 percent. Moreover, you can alter these threshold levels at any time to adapt to variations in sales capacity or business conditions.

Of course, as discussed in Chapter 12, leads that turn out not to be sales ready, and those that get stalled somewhere in the sales process, should be recycled for further nurturing and development until they are ready to come back around again, at the right time. A lead is a terrible thing to waste.

Many companies use the term "Marketing Qualified Leads" (MQLs) for those leads identified though lead scoring and then passed on from marketing to sales. These leads can be passed directly on to quota-carrying sales reps. But companies with more sophisticated RPM processes often introduce an intermediate step of lead qualification. We'll take a look at these final steps in the revenue cycle in the next chapter.

KEY POINTS

- Fewer than a quarter of early-stage buyers whose contact information has been captured by marketing are actually sales-ready.

- Prematurely turning leads over to sales can both alienate potential customers and aggravate the historical friction between sales and marketing.

- Lead nurturing cultivates, tracks, and maintains contact with leads to the point where they either become sales-ready or have opted out of the process. It involves communications in both directions and is most effective when individualized to each buyer.

- Scoring helps to focus the sales team's efforts on those prospects most likely to buy, particularly when the scoring system is the joint product of both sales and marketing.

CHAPTER 18

Making Every Sales Moment Count

In 2006, then Vice President Dick Cheney had an unfortunate hunting accident on a ranch in Texas during which he shot a friend in the face. Fortunately, the victim's injuries were not life threatening, and the main upshot of the incident was to provide fodder for late-night television comedians. Personally, though, I found a less well-known aspect of the incident to be both more interesting and a lot more humorous: The property on which the Vice President was hunting was a specially stocked quail ranch, chock full of not-quite-wild birds on tap for high-efficiency hunting. It's amazing how far hunting has come from the lonely Masai warrior, who was forced to stalk the Serengeti for days at a time to feed his family.

And yes, the Vice President's high-speed quail hunt really does have something to do with Revenue Performance Management. Remember the lonely hunter we met in Chapter 2, not in the Serengeti, but out in the sales field in hunt of the deal? Like the spear-to-mouth life of the Masai warrior, the sales hunter's life can also be wildly unproductive. Consider the following statistics:

- 94 percent of all Marketing Qualified Leads will never close (source: SiriusDecisions).

- Sales representatives spend 68 percent of their time on administration and preparation, not talking to customers (source: IDC).

- The average sales team will make 1,000 telephone calls to close one sale (source: "Cold Calling Dead or Alive" by Doyle Slayton).

- 52 percent of sales representatives in the United States did not achieve their sales quotas in 2010 (source: CSO Insights).

This is the sad state of creating revenue during the second decade of the twenty-first century, a state wherein the marketing and sales process is characterized by tremendous waste and inefficiency. Marketing spends money to create leads that salespeople too often ignore or squander, all the while wasting their own time unproductively "dialing for dollars."

It's a wonder there aren't more salespeople deciding to throw in the towel and move to the Serengeti.

FROM THE SERENGETI TO THE SUPERMARKET

But there's an alternative, one that's highlighted by these same sorry sales statistics. In order to change the situation and increase revenue efficiency, organizations must improve the productivity of their front line sales teams.

Just as the well-stocked Texas ranch offers a vast improvement in "hunting productivity" over wandering through the Serengeti, a sales team well stocked with leads can achieve significant improvements in productivity, quota attainment, and revenue production. The percentage will vary widely depending on the type of business, but it's safe to say that mature, profitable businesses spend between 15 and 40 percent of revenue on their sales organizations. That percentage is even higher in earlier stage, high-growth companies. Because the cost of sales is such a large part of what organizations spend, even small improvements in the efficiency of the sales process can have significant top-line and bottom-line impact and generate growth.

If your sales representatives can spend 20 or even just 10 percent more of their time talking to positively inclined and motivated prospects, instead of cold calling or wasting that time on unproductive territory administration, they will radically improve their quota achievement and booked revenue results. And the good news is that we now know exactly how to make it happen.

When marketing adopts effective processes for awareness building, inbound marketing, lead nurturing, and lead scoring using methods that they've shaped around buyers' needs, they are able to supply a continuous stream of well-qualified leads to their sales colleagues. And once sales realizes the value of this new generation of nurtured leads, their inherently acquisitive—some might even say greedy—nature will lead them to stop wasting and start embracing marketing-originated leads.

The systematic revenue processes described earlier in this book don't come to a screeching halt whenever a lead is passed from marketing to sales. After all, we in the Western world don't feed ourselves by visiting a high-productivity hunting ranch a couple of times a week; we drive to the local supermarket and buy our chickens neatly trimmed and (over-) packaged in plastic. Sales teams shouldn't revert to their primal hunting instincts either. Instead, they need to strive for the same consistently high level of productivity. And it's achievable.

Three additional processes—lead qualification with a human touch, sales prioritization, and lead recycling—extend the revenue productivity improvements available to marketing and carry them directly into the heart of the sales department. In this chapter, we'll look at each of these in turn.

THE HIGH-EFFICIENCY HUMAN TOUCH

Great things happen when marketing hands qualified leads—identified by a lead scoring process—directly to front-line sales representatives; that is, as long as salespeople take them seriously and follow up promptly.

Notwithstanding all the benefits of a well-designed, sophisticated, highly automated, lead nurturing and scoring process, it turns out that these processes are far from perfect. We're dealing with people, after all; and we can't describe their motivations, intentions, and behaviors using a simple numeric score. So, short of trying to capture every aspect of human thought and emotion in one comprehensive metric, we can often significantly improve sales efficiency by adopting a rigorous process of sales lead qualification. The goal is to have your quota-carrying sales reps spend their valuable time with the best of the best. And that involves taking leads that marketing has determined are well qualified, and further qualifying them through the human touch.

The human touch, in this case, comes in the form of a *sales development* process. Here, a team of lower-cost, highly disciplined, and well-trained specialists works to further qualify leads before they are passed to quota-carrying account executives. These specialists, called Sales Development Representatives, or SDRs, use telephone, e-mail, and other personal one-to-one interactions with prospective buyers to really get a pulse of "who's hot and who's not."

Inserting a sales development team between marketing and front-line sales actually offers several advantages in creating a high-performance revenue machine:

- *Better, faster, more consistent follow-up on leads.* You don't want a sales rep to call a marketing-qualified lead once, leave a voice-mail, get busy with another deal, and then fail to follow up. Yet this scenario happens all the time. And even if the sales rep follows up dutifully, you don't want to delay and give your competitors a chance to respond first. You want someone whose sole job in life is to reach your leads as quickly as possible, overcome their objections, make sure they're a fit, and connect them to your sales team.

- *Better sales effectiveness.* You want your salespeople to spend their time closing business with qualified customers, not on educating raw leads, talking to people who don't want to talk to them or, even worse, talking to tire-kickers and other unqualified prospects. Yet, try as you might, these kinds of people will still find their way through the best lead-scoring process. So it makes much more sense to have lower-cost SDRs talking to leads and then passing only the real ones onto sales.

- *Scalable human touch enhances the number of buyers you can serve.* Sales cycles take real time and energy. Even the best sales reps can only provide good service to a certain number of prospects at any one time. And often when they try doing more, they actually end up producing less. A scalable, lower-cost SDR team allows you to provide more of that human touch to prospects. Slightly less mature leads can remain in the SDRs' care and then be passed to a sales rep at the perfect moment.

- *Superior data.* Marketing and sales managers frequently complain that salespeople don't update information about leads in their CRM tool; indeed this is a criticism that's largely justified. It's much easier to require SDRs to enter proper information. This will give marketing more accurate information that they can use to optimize future lead nurturing and lead scoring efforts.

- *Minimize error.* It's relatively inexpensive for an SDR to call an incremental lead, but the opportunity cost of missing out on a deal can potentially be very high. Having a sales development function that sits between marketing and front-line sales allows a company to avoid having sales engage with leads who aren't yet ready ("false positives"), while at the same time reducing the risk of missing out on real potential deals ("false negatives").

- *Talent development.* Your sales development reps can play an important role in your sales talent pipeline, effectively becoming your farm team for future quota-carrying reps. They give you the opportunity to bring on new sales talent that already understands your business, is proven to work in your culture, and who knows your processes and cadence from day one. In a world where one in three sales hires fail, an SDR function can greatly reduce your hiring risk.

In sum, a well-managed sales development team can form an essential bridge between the high-volume automated processes used by a company's demand marketing team to find, nurture, and score its early stage prospects, on the one hand, and the highly skilled personal interactions between sales representatives and qualified buyers, on the other.

ALWAYS BE PRIORITIZING

Sales can be a frustratingly herky-jerky operation in many companies. Buyers come and go; they cancel and reschedule meetings, and make new and unusual demands. They manage to keep even the best sales reps on their toes, oscillating between feast and famine every day of their jobs. So in order to achieve any sort of reasonable productivity, let alone exceed their quotas, sales reps must always be working on more deals than they can reasonably expect to close. Sales managers call this "pipeline coverage," a situation where sales teams often work on 4 to 10 times as many deals as they'll actually close in that particular month or quarter. The same factors come into play in a sales development team, whose members should always be talking with the greatest number of leads they can efficiently manage.

So, in what has become a recurring theme across the entire revenue cycle, sales personnel not only need to "always be closing" and "always be helping," but also need to "always be prioritizing." To put it more bluntly, sales professionals achieve maximum efficiency when they can cherry-pick among opportunities and allocate their time to the very best.

I realize that this sounds like heresy to some sales leaders. The problem of the prima donna sales rep—who only cherry picks and doesn't dig in and do the hard work—is legendary. However, this turns upside down when sales take place in the context of a comprehensive Revenue Performance Management process. The entire process in this scheme is centered on the notion of cherry picking. It starts by planting the most seeds—that is, as many early stage prospects as possible—and then filtering, scoring, and prioritizing at every subsequent step of the process. As long as you plant enough seeds, everyone along the revenue process has the luxury of picking the best ones. And if it they can do so accurately, on average and over time, revenue magic happens.

This is partly because sales teams can repurpose the same sorts of digital marketing tools that marketing uses to implement effective lead scoring processes, using them to prioritize salespeople's own time. Remember, lead scoring is all about continuously monitoring and evaluating who the best leads are by considering demographic data, company profile data, and near real-time buyer behavior, such as visiting a website, clicking a link, or attending an online event.

Every day, when a salesperson walks into the office or prepares for a road trip, he or she must decide how to allocate their time. Who to call first? Who to visit this week? Part of the art and science of sales involves making these decisions accurately. When you have more information at hand, you can probably make a better decision. And since so much of the buying process takes place online these days, there is a wealth of new information to harness that can help salespeople better allocate their time.

Buyers are constantly interacting with web pages, social media sites, videos, online events, and other information resources that influence their purchase decisions. Today's new generation of sales tools can monitor, measure, and analyze these buyer behaviors and interactions; summarize them for quick consumption; and then place that information directly into the CRM systems that salespeople use every day to support their work. This means that when a salesperson looks at their

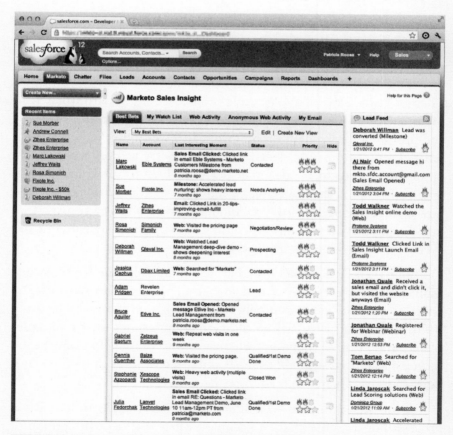

FIGURE 18.1   A sales priority dashboard empowers sales personnel to make decisions about where to spend their time with just a quick glance.
Source: © copyright salesforce.com, inc. Used with permission.

CRM system, they don't just see a list of names and phone numbers. They also receive active guidance about which of their prospects are hot *right now*.

Sales reps who take these cues and make their first phone call or customer visit based on this sort of priority guidance can direct their scarce time to the people most likely to buy soonest. Of course, no system can guarantee perfection. But salespeople play the odds, and those who choose to allocate their time to buyers showing the most engagement will be more productive.

IT'S EASY BEING GREEN

Of course, no matter how well a sales team qualifies prospects and prioritizes its time, stuff happens. Herky-jerky buyers come and go, sometimes forever but often only for a few weeks or months.

Traditionally, salespeople who hear "not now" from a prospect, whether at the start of a sales cycle or after weeks of hard work, tend to do one of two things: shuffle the lead off to some private purgatory and promptly forget about it, or engage in a well-practiced exercise of self-delusion or outright denial wherein they try to keep working the opportunity until their sales manager tells them to get real and stop. The end result is that a very large number of prospects who say "not now" end up being lost forever. And it doesn't come as a surprise that salespeople end up picking one of these two options, since no one has ever given them a better alternative.

But there *is* a better way. Any complete Revenue Performance Management process needs to embrace the idea of *lead recycling*: the process by which sales routinely hands leads that have strayed away from the buying path back to marketing, entrusting their colleagues to take good care of them. In turn, marketing commits to bringing the recycled lead back around to sales if and when the lead shifts from "not now" back to "Okay, I'm ready."

Lead recycling can be quite nuanced in a sophisticated RPM process. For example, marketing might offer sales reps the option of recycling a lead back to marketing for one month, or one quarter, or even indefinitely, all with the understanding that they'll reintroduce the lead if they ever show renewed buying signals. These shorter-term options give salespeople the ability to offload the responsibility for staying in touch when a buyer hits the pause button for a short period, while the indefinite option accommodates more serious and lengthy delays in the buying process. Even better, modern CRM and RPM systems only require the salesperson to click one or two buttons to complete the whole recycling process. These tools allow them to maximize the amount of time they spend on active buyers, without ignoring slower sales cycles that still require attention.

It takes a lot of trust for a salesperson to hand a real lead back to marketing, even if it's not an urgent one. The salesperson might wonder if he will ever see it again. But when marketing and sales have achieved a measure of mutual trust around the lead lifecycle, the results can be very powerful. When marketing receives a lead recycled back from sales, they use the same lead nurturing concept that applies to new leads. But this time it includes specialized "keep warm" programs to maintain continuity of the buying relationship, and to detect reenergized buyer interest that immediately reignites the sales cycle.

With this kind of lead recycling process in place, many companies with more advanced RPM programs find that as many as 30 percent of all their sales opportunities flow back through the recycling process, from sales to marketing. And a substantial percentage of those return to sales at a later date as renewed sales opportunities. Without RPM, most of the opportunities that flow through this cycle would instead be lost forever. Lead recycling brings these short-term and long-term dormant leads back to life, sometimes as closed revenue. It's almost like found money, dropping straight to the bottom line.

Understand the Revenue Lifecycle

Through the past four chapters, we have taken a low-level flyover of the entire revenue process that went from defining terms and laying a foundation, to early stage awareness building; content-driven inbound marketing; lead capture, nurturing, and scoring; and then on to the front lines of efficient sales. One thing should be clear by now: There are literally dozens of points where a systematically planned and executed revenue process can radically improve marketing and sales efficiency, increase effectiveness, and open the door to accelerated growth and business performance.

But, as in the case of a complex manufacturing operation or a global real-time supply chain, this is neither a simple process nor one that you can implement and then ignore. Each of the processes described here can yield benefits when executed in simple form. But continuously improving them will guarantee that they continue to yield sustained improvements in revenue efficiency and growth.

The key to capturing this sort of sustained improvement is revenue analytics. Each of the process steps involved in generating revenue can be monitored and measured, improved, and perfected. And beyond simply tuning a high-performance machine, revenue analytics opens the door to the future: Once a well-defined and well-measured revenue process is in place, revenue analytics can help to project future revenue in a way that has never before been possible. In the next chapter, we'll look at how to turn all the efficiencies achieved through RPM into strategic insights and revenue growth.

KEY POINTS

- Sales costs are among the greatest expenses for any business, so even marginal improvements in sales efficiency can have a dramatic impact on booked revenue.

- Improving the quality and quantity of leads that sales departments receive will translate into much higher sales team productivity.

- A sales development team, situated between demand marketing and sales, can provide prospects with an essential human touch while further qualifying potential leads.

- More and better information about prospects can lead to better, more effective processes throughout the revenue cycle.

- Leads that have temporarily fallen away from the revenue path should be recycled, not lost.

CHAPTER 19

Shining a Bright Light on the Revenue Machine

In business, as in politics and warfare, information is power. The ability to rapidly collect, accurately analyze, and promptly act on information makes the difference between triumph and failure. In fact, according to a study from MIT's Sloan School of Management, companies that use "data-driven decision making" achieved productivity levels 5 to 6 percent higher than could be explained by other factors. Simply put, decisions based on "data and analysis" result in better revenue growth than those based on the traditional management arts of "experience and intuition." Analytics offers one of the most powerful levers available to produce more predictable, sustainable revenue performance, along with significantly improved bottom line results.

Analytics also drive continuous improvement. The change required for Revenue Performance Management is a process for which companies must establish key metrics. They must then apply analytics to those metrics as part of a continuous, systematic effort to find ways to improve. And although each individual improvement might only be a fraction of a percent, those changes aggregate into striking progress over time.

The right analytics can help organizations turn raw RPM data into knowledge about optimizing each stage of the revenue process. They can range from tactical analytics that help marketing practitioners make better day-to-day decisions about how to allocate investments across different programs and campaigns, to highly strategic analytics that provide a complete, end-to-end view of how revenue is flowing across the full revenue cycle, including forecasts into the future.

Of course, analytic tools can also provide useful snapshots of revenue health and performance. Indeed, any complete Revenue Performance Management system will include ad hoc reporting and analysis tools that give revenue and financial professionals unprecedented insights into their revenue machine. But on a journey of continuous improvement, it is also essential that the organization identifies and adopts a stable set of metrics, ones they can use to measure and compare essential parameters on an apples-to-apples basis over time. Such metrics are often called Key Performance Indicators (KPIs), and there is a sophisticated body of knowledge and best practices regarding the use of KPIs in the domains of manufacturing, quality, supply chain, and corporate governance.

KPIs are much less evolved in the revenue domain. But in a post-Enron, post-Sarbanes-Oxley world, boards, CEOs and CFOs are demanding that revenue processes be accorded the same precision of measurement and degree of accountability as these other domains.

I vividly recall a story from several years ago. I was talking to the CMO at a well-known, high-flying technology company who told me, "I was literally reduced to tears in our last company board meeting. The board started demanding that I produce numbers showing how my marketing activities were impacting revenue. Once they got their teeth into this topic, they wouldn't stop. I couldn't respond, because my team didn't produce numbers like that. But the worst part wasn't that I didn't have actual numbers to share with the board. It was that I didn't know what metrics I should even be reporting against to give them a meaningful answer." Such is the sorry state of revenue analytics.

That's why this chapter looks at the revenue performance metrics and KPIs that revenue leaders in every company should track to diagnose the health of their revenue process and to optimize results over time. Beyond using metrics to track what has already happened, we'll also explore the leading indicators that help organizations forecast future revenue results.

THE END OF "HALF MY MARKETING IS WASTED"

Measuring the contribution that a given marketing program has on revenue and profits has long been the holy grail of marketing—and revenue—analysis, ever since John Wanamaker's famous quip dating from around the turn of the century: "Half of the money I spend on advertising is wasted; the trouble is, I don't know which half." Oh, and by "turn of the century" I mean the *last* century as in the year 1900!

But believe it or not, I hear somebody uttering a version of this hundred-year-old canard every week or so. Public speakers at marketing conferences open with that line all the time, sometimes acting as if it is a fresh new anecdote. I'm sick of it, and I have made it my personal mission in life to kill off this phrase once and for all.

While it's admittedly not as clever or euphonic, my goal is to replace Wanamaker's quip with this:

Almost none of my marketing and sales investment is wasted, but I can easily find out which aspects are performing least well, and make rapid adjustments to drive more revenue.

The advent of the Internet, Google, social media, and all the other digital innovations has prompted the data universe to explode like a supernova over the past 10 or 15 years. At the same time, the ability to use analytics to comb through mountains of data and glean important insights has also radically advanced. Today, it is possible to apply advanced analytics to understand exactly what marketing expenditures and programs have the most impact, both on acquiring customers and moving them down the pipeline.

One reason for the elusive progress in this area is that few people have really taken the time to understand the complexity of the problem, or create solutions that address that complexity. Instead, they keep reaching for simple answers to problems that aren't simple at all.

It's worth taking a minute to illustrate this. Let's explore one apparently simple question: "What is the revenue impact of a trade show that marketing attended last month, at a cost of $100,000?" There are some real complexities here.

- *Accounting for time.* The impact that the money you invest in marketing today has on buyers will be unclear, and will occur at uncertain points in the future. Last month's trade show may deliver results next month, or maybe not for another two years. But marketers need to decide where to invest their budget today. Moreover, marketing investments like trade shows don't yield payback all at one time. Leads that you initially found at last year's trade show could still become customers at some point in the future.

- *Multiple touches.* Any complex or high value sale requires multiple interactions—10, 20, even 50—between buyer and seller to move from a cold lead to closed business. And these interactions vary; they might be web visits, e-mails, phone calls, live events, and so on. Yet CMOs get asked all the time questions like, "How many opportunities did you generate from that $100,000 you spent on a last month's trade show?" Those same CMOs end up digging a deeper hole for themselves by producing naïve answers to this kind of question, answers that completely miss the nuance of multiple touches. The trade show itself may not have generated any opportunities at all, but it probably did exert a positive influence on many prospective buyers.

- *Multiple influencers.* The buying committee for a major purchase can involve five, ten, or even several dozen people. Different marketing programs affect each individual differently, so it is a constant challenge to determine which programs have the most impact. Some of the buying team members involved with a deal might have attended the trade show; others probably did not.

- *Extraneous variables.* In many cases, there are factors outside the revenue team's control that significantly impact results, from macroeconomic trends, to the weather, to the quality of sales reps. Did revenues increase because the economy improved? Or should marketers claim that their trade show deserves all the credit? Or was it just a sunny day that prompted people to get out of the house?

These factors illustrate how difficult it is to gain an accurate understanding of revenue cycle dynamics. Variables like time, people, environment, and interacting events introduce complexities that challenge our ability to produce simple answers to what *appear* to be simple questions. Many CEOs, CFOs, financial planning professionals and others have never been fully educated about these complexities, so they probably don't understand that they're asking the wrong questions in the first place. And while many CMOs intuitively understand the complexity of their world, they haven't been taught how to discuss its revenue aspects in analytic terms. So they resort to giving simplistic answers that don't satisfy anyone.

Fortunately, there are new leading-edge revenue analytic tools that can help untangle this mess. Their foundation is an end-to-end Revenue Performance Management concept that spans the full buying cycle across marketing and sales. Within this RPM framework, each company formulates its own Revenue Cycle Model, which sets down a structure to track interactions and take consistent measurements as the buying process unfolds for each prospective customer.

The RPM process, and the Revenue Cycle Model embedded in it, captures outcomes: How many leads did we generate in the last quarter? How many web page visits happened? How many new sales opportunities did we create? How many people did we meet at the trade show? And how much revenue did the sales team produce last quarter? RPM also tracks investments in revenue generation: How much did each marketing program cost? Which leads did that program "touch" in a meaningful way? How much did we invest in sales commissions to capture that revenue?

By bringing together comprehensive information about investments and outcomes that span the entire revenue cycle, true ROI analysis becomes possible. Yet I would venture to guess that fewer than 1 percent of corporations today have this information available at all, let alone organized and correlated in this way. But achieving this goal is the ultimate reward for adopting a Revenue Performance Management strategy. To get there, CFOs, CMOs (and Chief Revenue Officers, as we'll discuss in Part IV) need to learn a new set of metrics. They'll need to look for new KPIs, and they'll need to cultivate the discipline to think about, talk about, and measure their marketing and sales investments using terminology and techniques akin to those used for more familiar capital investments.

TREATING MARKETING LIKE AN INVESTMENT

A company that can think about creating revenue in hard ROI terms will start to see marketing less as a cost center and more as an investment in revenue generation. This idea not only applies at the conceptual level, it also manifests itself in concrete detail when planning and evaluating how much money to spend on various marketing programs. CFOs and other metric-savvy executives are already comfortable with this kind of investment analysis in other contexts. For example, when making a decision about a major capital equipment purchase, or building a new factory, or opening a new branch store, financial analysts frequently deal with point-in-time investments that yield predictable returns, but over an uncertain period of time. Yet these same people frequently fail to apply this kind of thinking to revenue. Instead, they ask the CMO a month after a trade show, "What did we get from it?" expecting a simple point-in-time answer. They would never ask this same kind of question the month after breaking ground on a new factory.

Of course, treating marketing like an investment also carries two key implications. The first is that any plan for a marketing investment needs to begin with a quantified set of expected outcomes: What are the best case, worst case, and expected case outcomes? And what do we expect will happen in return for this money we want to spend?

The second, more controversial, implication is that marketing investments should be amortized over the useful life of that expense. Marketing investments usually do not yield immediate returns; rather, they often come months or years down the road. The principle of matching expenses against the revenue generated by those expenses implies that marketing investments should be capitalized as assets, not treated like simple expense items. In other words, the money that companies spend on marketing should be amortized over the entire period in which they deliver benefit to the organization. I believe that someday, financial standards boards like FASB and IASB will figure this out and begin to mandate this kind of financial thinking.

GO WITH THE FLOW: MEASURING THE REVENUE CYCLE

The typical sales executive does not lack for metrics reflecting the health of the sales cycle. Every CEO knows and understands KPIs like average selling price and win rate. But RPM is all about transforming the ways marketing and sales work, and work together. So it requires a new set of metrics that focus not on how well marketing or sales are doing on their own, but on the overall effectiveness and efficiency of the end-to-end revenue machine. This, in turn, requires a different and broader set of KPIs to monitor and optimize the health of the revenue funnel.

Strategic KPIs for revenue evaluate the overall performance and efficiency of the complete revenue cycle. They are the primary criteria by which companies measure continuous process improvement, and they can warn executives early on about potential problems or opportunities regarding future revenue. Some of these include:

- *Customer Acquisition Cost.* The best way to measure the overall effectiveness of your revenue process is to measure total revenue (or bookings, or gross margin) generated, divided by the total amount spent on marketing and sales. The details of how to calculate this metric will vary widely for different kinds of businesses. But its high level objective is to net out investments in revenue across the entire marketing and sales cycle, and to match those investments against revenue earned in order to come up with a single overall measure of revenue productivity. In this case, the lower that number, the better.

- *Pipeline Contribution from Marketing.* No matter how well elaborated a company's end-to-end RPM process might be, at the end of the quarter, some new business will be attributable to the efforts of marketing and its seed nurturing and lead nurturing programs. Other revenue will be tied directly to sales, through partners, channels, or other avenues. RPM's core message is this: On average, much more revenue should be attributed to marketing than its historical averages, because that revenue is generated more efficiently, at lower cost, and with more scalability. So another essential KPI is the percentage of total revenue contribution that comes from marketing. In general, higher is better here.

- *Inventory of Active Prospects and Opportunities.* The current inventories of active names, prospects, leads, and opportunities in your revenue funnel represent your pool of future customers. Tracking the relative balance of these inventories, and their changes over time, shows the revenue pipeline's overall health and forms the basis for long-range forecasting. Inventories of early-stage, less-well-qualified leads will, of course, be larger than late-stage qualified leads or opportunities. However, a KPI that measures the relative size of these inventories over time can be a valuable early alert to changes in corporate revenue dynamics that merit further analysis.

- *ROMI (Return on Marketing Investment).* It's not enough just to know that a marketing program generated lots of leads. By allocating revenue and gross margin to specific buyer touches and calculating the net return on investment, organizations can begin to get a much clearer picture of their optimal portfolio of marketing investments.

Underlying these strategic KPIs, which should be visible to the CEO, CFO, and even the board of directors, is a range of metrics that are highly relevant to members of the revenue team. These are used by the CMO, the head of demand marketing, and other revenue leaders to plan, assess effectiveness, and suggest improvements. As described in Figure 19.1, there are four categories of RPM "metrics that matter"

Metric	Questions It Will Answer	Examples
Flow (Lead Generation)	How many people entered each pipeline stage in a given period? Are these trending up or down?	How many new prospects were created last month? How many marketing-qualified leads did we pass along last week?
Balance (Lead Counts)	How many people are in each pipeline stage? How many accounts? Do they vary by lead type? Are their numbers going up or down over time?	How many active prospects do I have—since the size of my prospect database is a key indicator of future success?
Conversion	What is the conversion ratio from stage to stage? Which types of leads have the best conversion rate?	Which (if any) of my conversion rates are trending up? Or down?
Velocity	What is the average "revenue cycle" time? How does it break down by stage?	Do certain types of leads move faster through the pipeline? How is their speed changing over time?

FIGURE 19.1   Four key categories of CRM metrics.

that can be used to assess the health of the revenue cycle: flow, balance, conversion, and velocity.

By tracking these metrics by stage, by business, and over time, revenue executives can plainly see what is actually happening with buyers, what may happen in the future, and which levers they need to pull in order to prompt buyers to buy.

THE POWER OF LONG-RANGE REVENUE FORECASTING

Although it's always important to look back in order to understand what worked and what didn't, it's even more important to look forward and deliver insight into what is *likely* to happen and what *will* work. Many companies rely on their sales forecasts. However, sales forecasts are based on assumptions about what specific accounts will do at specific times. This usually means that the further out you look, the more speculative and inaccurate they become. The shorter the sales cycle, the worse the problem. And the fact that buyers engage with sales increasingly later and later in that process just aggravates the problem further.

However, marketing executives can develop vastly more visibility into future period revenues as they take more responsibility for early revenue cycle stages. They can use statistical tools to forecast how many new leads, new opportunities, and how much end-to-end revenue their machine will yield in future periods. That's because they know exactly how many prospects are in each revenue cycle stage and how likely those prospects are to move through each stage over time.

REVENUE REVOLUTIONARIES

Egencia®, an Expedia, Inc. Company

As the corporate travel arm of Expedia, Inc., the world's leading travel company, Egencia is the fifth largest travel management company in the world. Egencia helps businesses succeed by offering the industry's only fully integrated corporate travel

(continued)

(*continued*)

service. Egencia's industry expertise helps companies increase their travel policy compliance, reduce their cost of business travel, and improve employee productivity. Egencia offers a complete corporate travel program supported by its expertise in the global travel market and a best-in-class technology platform. To carry its revenues to new levels of profitable growth, Egencia has now embraced a Revenue Performance Management (RPM) approach to its marketing and sales functions.

CHALLENGES

Egencia's marketing team understood there were multiple "pain points" in their process that they needed to address. "We were out there looking for an ice cube, but instead we found an iceberg," as one team member put it. However, fixing those longstanding issues also presented a major opportunity to improve the company's marketing infrastructure for better long-term results. The marketing function within Egencia had been operating in a sort of "bubble," disconnected from sales and operations. At the same time, the marketing group found it very difficult to tie its activities back to a tangible return on investment (ROI). This absence of ROI metrics did not help the team's efforts to win essential support for expanding its marketing budget. Also, on the demand generation front, Egencia faced the classic problems of too little visibility, low accuracy on leads, a focus on campaign quantity at the expense of much-needed quality, and painfully slow response times in campaign execution.

SOLUTION

Following an exhaustive market and technology assessment, Egencia adopted a fully integrated RPM solution, encompassing marketing automation, sales effectiveness, and revenue analytics technologies. The company's aim was to achieve a major transformation of its marketing activities in order to deliver greater, more sustainable, and measurable revenue results.

BENEFITS

With RPM powering the company's new revenue engine, Egencia's marketing efforts became automated, optimized, and seamlessly connected to other marketing, sales, and operational activities.

Perhaps the most important benefit was the new level of coordination between the company's marketing, sales, and agency operations. By using RPM, Egencia was finally able to get its essential revenue-related functions to work together and produce results that had previously been unheard of. "It was no longer us versus them," one marketing team member said. "As a result of our adopting RPM, sales and marketing now share the load. That has created a much more seamless, efficient, and ultimately successful approach to the revenue process."

Jennifer O'Brien, Director of Marketing at Egencia says, "With our new Revenue Performance Management solution, we are now able to tangibly demonstrate to senior management the ROI of our actions. Equally important, we now have critical visibility on what is working, and what isn't. As such, we can shift precious marketing resources to those activities that actually move the revenue needle for Egencia."

Source: Egencia®. Used with permission.

Extending revenue forecast accuracy further forward in time is hugely valuable to business leaders. More revenue visibility gives executives more time to react in good times and bad. In a bad-news scenario, an indication of pipeline softness several quarters in advance of the point where traditional sales forecasts lose accuracy can be invaluable. Executives can increase investments in marketing and sales to compensate, or slow hiring and cut other costs in a deliberate and measured way to manage profitability. In a good-news scenario, long-range revenue forecasts can help executives to seize opportunities. For example, if early-stage lead inventories are increasing but future sales hiring plans are static, executives may want to move quickly to add sales capacity to capture that pending growth.

In Chapter 13, I talked about how marketing leaders are often overlooked in a company's forecast process—and as integral contributors to revenue. The longer-range revenue forecasting that Revenue Performance Management enables can alter this dynamic. If the CMO can come to the revenue table with hard, defensible, actionable forecasts about future revenue, I guarantee that people will listen.

This is a fundamentally new role for marketing, and it may not come easily in some organizations. Marketers may resist measurement, perhaps because accountability is a double-edged sword: it shines a bright light on both high-quality and poor performance. But the trend is inevitable. RPM makes the data and technology available to give C-suite executives the insights into revenue and marketing program metrics that they have long desired.

KEY POINTS

- Key Performance Indicators, or KPIs, are the essential metrics of business processes. However, companies rarely use them to full effect when measuring marketing and revenue generation activities.

- Measuring the impact of marketing investments is complicated by factors like time, external forces, multiple interactions, and various individuals influencing a sale.

- The RPM concept and its company-specific Revenue Cycle Models capture outcome metrics that can be paired with investment data to yield true ROI information.

- Justifications for marketing investments need to specify their expected outcomes over the life of their benefit to the company.

- Strategic KPIs for revenue include customer acquisition cost, pipeline contributions from marketing, inventory of active prospects, and return on marketing investment.

- Key RPM metrics involve lead generation, lead counts at each stage, conversion rates, and velocity.

- RPM enables more accurate revenue forecasts and allows executives to adjust their spending priorities accordingly.

CHAPTER 20

Technology for the Revenue Process

You may have noticed that I've hardly said anything about technology and systems—until this point. That was intentional. The business transformation and continuous improvement that Revenue Performance Management requires isn't about deploying a new technology system. It is about people, processes, metrics, creative content, and a culture of continuous improvement. But, as with almost any aspect of modern life, we need technology to support the business processes involved with RPM.

In principle, managers at GE could keep their books without an ERP system, and just use ledger books and an army of accountants. But today, even the smallest businesses no longer use manual methods to keep their books, given the abundance of inexpensive, easy-to-use software available for that purpose.

The same basic idea applies to Revenue Performance Management. Since we are talking about digital marketing—websites, Google search, social media, e-mail, and the like—there are going to be computers and software involved in the process. But in concept, a company could implement most of the business processes described in Part III of this book using largely manual methods. They could capture new leads acquired from inbound marketing and store them in spreadsheets or on a personal database such as Microsoft Access. A legion of marketers could review the leads every day, deciding whom to keep in touch with as part of their lead nurturing programs, and then calculate and update the scores for all those leads. Once a lead is qualified for sales, the marketer could type out an e-mail and send the contact information over to a sales rep. But having a legion of marketers to do that makes no more sense than for GE to keep their books with an army of accountants.

Yet amazingly, many companies today are still trying to cope with the world of online digital marketing using exactly these sorts of manual methods. Over the past few years, I have personally worked with dozens of companies, including ones with revenues in excess of $1 billion, who are drowning under a tidal wave of online leads that has overwhelmed their traditional manual processes.

WHY DOES REVENUE PERFORMANCE MANAGEMENT NEED A SYSTEM?

I was lucky to be born at a date early enough that I can remember comedienne Lucille Ball at her prime. She was about the funniest person on earth. To this day, I remember a scene from an iconic episode of *I Love Lucy* in which Lucy and her best friend, Ethel Mertz, get a job at a candy factory, working on an assembly line, boxing chocolates. At first they keep up with the pace of the assembly line, but as it goes faster and faster and faster, mayhem breaks out. Lucy and Ethel resort to all sorts of crazy antics—storing the chocolates in their mouths, hats, even shirts—to cope with the deluge of candy, until the whole thing collapses in a bout of hysterics.

Whenever I think about modern inbound marketing processes, I always find myself thinking about that scene from *I Love Lucy*. It's pretty obvious why: When you first start publishing powerful content online, engaging with buyers on social media, and using SEO and SEM to attract interest, the results can be gratifying. New leads start streaming through the door in an almost assembly line progression. The assembly line starts moving faster and faster and faster as you improve in search optimization and invest more in your marketing programs. Sooner or later, mayhem breaks out. But it's really not very funny. You end up throwing valuable leads on the floor.

So the first reason we need technology is due to the scale of the challenge. In a business of any size, especially one with an engaging web and social media presence, buyer interactions can number in the thousands, millions, or even hundreds of millions per week. A well-executed pay-per-click ad program on Google can generate thousands

FIGURE 20.1   An iconic episode of *I Love Lucy* evokes the challenges of managing a flow of leads from successful inbound marketing.
Source: © Getty Images. Used with permission.

of clicks in no time flat—clicks you need to capture and convert if you're going to transmute the money you invest with Google into revenue for your company. But without the right tools to automate the planning, operational execution, and measurement of RPM processes, even the hardest-working marketer will be overwhelmed.

Second, we have talked at length about how RPM is a *business process*—a sequence of steps and decisions that marketing and sales professionals make in a structured way. It's one thing to capture online leads and stuff them into a spreadsheet or a database or even a sales force automation system. But such an *ad hoc* approach is not a sustainable process. Instead, RPM calls for defined, repeatable business processes at the macro scale—steps that affect the entire revenue cycle of a corporation. RPM also facilitates the more detailed tactical processes of nurturing and developing relationships with each individual lead. Without technology, both types of processes will be significantly slower and more prone to error, making it virtually impossible to be sure that all members of the organization are following the right procedures.

Finally, as we saw in the previous chapter, analytics are critical for building credibility and continuously optimizing the revenue process. Those analytics depend on data. If you don't build a dedicated information system as the foundation for RPM, the data you generate during process execution is left in silos or lost forever, which you just cannot afford. The revenue process generates a profoundly valuable, but vast, amount of data. The right technology infrastructure allows you to collect, store, and maintain that data with appropriate privacy rights. You can then analyze it in ways that drive front-line revenue effectiveness, large-scale business insights, continuous revenue process improvements, and growth. In short, it's impossible to adopt all of the operational and analytic processes of RPM on the scale of modern business without a technology system.

You may be asking, "Isn't CRM this system?" The answer is— not really. While CRM is an essential tool for helping any modern sales organization keep track of buyers and lead contact information, it does not come with either the process model or the other capabilities required to automate the end-to-end revenue cycle.

At the most basic level, CRM is an accounting system. But instead of tracking a company's general ledger of financial transactions, it is an accounting system for people, tracking names and phone numbers. By itself, CRM doesn't deliver the capabilities needed for inbound marketing or seed nurturing; after all, you don't have any names or contact information to track at that stage. CRM doesn't automate lead qualification, lead nurturing, or lead lifecycle management, either, and it provides only a limited view into the detailed information about what's working, or not working, in the marketing department. Finally, CRM systems do not allow organizations to model their entire revenue processes across marketing and sales, collect essential performance data over time, or turn that data into strategic insights about revenue.

But there's also good news: An entirely new generation of online business applications has emerged over the past five years, one that's been specifically created to address the operational and analytic needs of Revenue Performance Management. Just as an entire industry of ERP providers sprouted up to help manage the supply chain, this new category of vendors provides RPM systems with the ability to manage the revenue chain. My company, Marketo, is one of several high-quality providers of such systems.

These RPM systems evolved from an earlier category of applications called Marketing Automation, or MA. And many MA capabilities remain integral to the broader and more capable RPM platforms. So understanding Marketing Automation is a good place to start.

MARKETING AUTOMATION: A CRITICAL STEP ON THE REVENUE JOURNEY

If you ask CFOs about their system of record, they'll point to an accounting or ERP system. If you ask sales VPs where their data sits, they'll point to the SFA or CRM system. Likewise, a VP of human resources and a VP of support, as well as most other business executives, will all have their own systems that provide the definitive view of their data and support the key processes for which they are responsible. But if you ask the CMO at most companies about their system of record, they'll probably mumble something about the CRM system, but ultimately point you to a variety of spreadsheets and ad hoc tools.

Over the past decade, more advanced marketing departments have begun to employ business applications called Marketing Automation, or MA. Marketing specialists use these applications to manage and automate the process of converting prospective customers into actual buyers. At its core, a Marketing Automation application is the system of record for early-stage leads, their profiles (job title, company size, etc.) and market-related behavior (website visits, tweets, e-mail clicks, etc.).

However, in addition to acting as the system of record for lead information, MA applications commonly include a wide array of other features and functions. Among them:

- E-mail marketing to communicate with customers and develop relationships by engaging them through multi-step campaigns.

- Social media marketing to automate engagement with social media users.

- Workflow and behavioral triggers to automate repetitive tasks such as following up with nonresponders or ensuring sales follow-up on prospects.

- Lead nurturing to help transform raw inquiries into sales-ready leads.

- Lead scoring to automate lead qualification and improve sales effectiveness by helping sales prioritize their time on the most promising opportunities.

- Lead management to automatically assign leads to the correct sales channel, ensure follow-up, and recycle as necessary.

- Event marketing to help maximize the ROI of webinars, trade shows, and other events

- Website monitoring to track prospect interactions online and identify which companies are hitting your site.

- Landing page optimization to make it easy to create, publish, and test web pages targeted at capturing leads.

Many Marketing Automation applications are rich with valuable features and functions. Yet, when companies start to think about adopting a comprehensive RPM strategy, the very name of this application category becomes its major weakness, because Marketing Automation is all about marketing. Although the best MA tools may integrate seamlessly with CRM and other systems that enable marketing to easily pass leads to sales without too much trouble, the fact remains that most people think of MA applications as living within the marketing department, supporting marketing processes, and storing only marketing data. They're regarded as tools that marketing department managers have purchased for their staff to use.

However, the last thing today's enterprises need is yet another silo of information, especially one that perpetuates and reinforces the long-standing disconnect between marketing and sales teams. The central theme of this book is worth mentioning here yet again: Marketing and sales need to reinvent and realign themselves into a single revenue machine. Enter the Revenue Performance Management platform.

A PLATFORM FOR CHANGE

Over the last few years, the best Marketing Automation applications have been reformulated in keeping with the reinvention that needs to take place within, as well as between, marketing and sales departments. The result is that a number of vendors have introduced strategic Revenue Performance Management platforms, which are comprehensive software systems that span marketing, sales, and finance; that support both operational and analytic business processes; and that fully enable the business processes needed for an RPM transformation.

Notice that I use the term *platform*, not *application*. I do this deliberately. Modern companies use hundreds if not thousands of software "applications." Some are small desktop tools, and some larger programs are used at the departmental or divisional level. But there are only a few that really merit the term *platform*: a software application that spans a significant range of business operations, used by personnel in multiple departments. It is a system of record, storing and managing important data used across the corporation. And it is a hub into which a variety of other applications and tools can be plugged to meet the company's unique business needs. One example of a platform is the ERP system, which might span and support manufacturing, supply chain, and finance. Now it's time for businesses to adopt an RPM platform.

But what does an RPM platform do? What are its essential elements? And how is it different from Marketing Automation?

At its core, the RPM platform cuts directly across marketing and sales, enabling continuous lead flows between the teams—forwarding them from marketing to sales, and then back again in the case of lead recycling. It is used every day by both marketing professionals and sales professionals who, as a result, are now looking at the same data, the same version of the truth. And because RPM is a platform, it is able to integrate with a wide variety of customer communication channels, including e-mail, SMS text messages, webinars, social media sites,

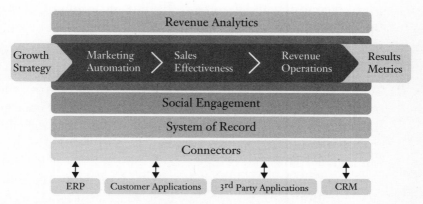

FIGURE 20.2 A Revenue Performance Management Platform spans marketing, sales, and finance. It supports the operational processes of RPM along with their strategic revenue analytics.

webinars and other online meetings, video, blogs, telephone, CRM systems, and more. RPM coordinates the two-way conversation with buyers across all of these channels, and it collects information from them for detailed analysis as well.

The evolution from a Marketing Automation system into a full, end-to-end RPM platform means adding, among other things:

- *Sales Productivity.* Chapter 18 explained how the single most important benefit of an RPM strategy is to help salespeople prioritize their time so they can spend more time with those prospective buyers who are the most highly qualified and ready to act. The RPM platform extends directly from marketing into sales, all the way to the front line sales rep. This means providing those reps with the insights they need to improve their sales time prioritization, and enabling smarter selling by letting reps know the right messages to deliver to each individual customer at the right times.

- *Business Process Modeling.* Earlier chapters looked at the Revenue Cycle Model, with its revenue stages and process steps that progressively move leads through a systematic sequence of phases from "seeds" into fully ripe sales opportunities. The RPM platform includes the tools required to model this revenue process around the unique circumstances of each company, and to support the ongoing evolution of that model over time.

- *Revenue Analytics.* The RPM platform integrates features to operate and manage revenue processes that span marketing and sales with the analytic capabilities needed to improve and optimize revenue over time. This includes reporting on core operations affecting revenue performance. But it also includes robust time-series analyses powered by a store of data that illuminate trends and compute such critical KPIs as lead-to-revenue flow, conversion rates, and lead velocity over time. RPM platforms can also provide tools to forecast pipeline and revenue for future periods and to model "what if" scenarios. For example, "What would be the revenue impact of a 10 percent budget increase next year?"

Perhaps the most significant trend in business application software over the past decade has been the shift to Software as a Service (SaaS), also known as cloud computing or on-demand applications. These are complete and robust business applications, delivered over the Internet, and accessed by users via a web browser. The benefits of this approach include lower up-front capital investment, faster implementation, and automatic upgrades whenever new capabilities are released. All of the RPM platforms on the market today use the SaaS delivery model; they also integrate with other SaaS applications, as well as with locally installed applications such as CRM and ERP.

Let me conclude this discussion of RPM platforms with two comments: First, I've characterized RPM as a platform for both marketing and sales, one which provides an important system of record that a variety of specialized disciplines and departments can use. But I must also acknowledge the fact that RPM systems are designed to augment, *not* replace, CRM. The best of them integrate and synchronize their data so that the revenue system of record is really the unified amalgamation of data from both CRM and RPM.

Second, the use of far-reaching terms like "platform" can be daunting, especially for smaller businesses. That's especially understandable because Revenue Performance Management systems span both marketing and sales, and they support operational processes as well as perform analytics. Yet today a number of vendors deliver RPM systems that are scaled for corporations of every size, from the world's largest enterprises to those with just 10 or 20 employees. Today's market includes an RPM platform choice appropriate for virtually every business.

Bill Gates once said, "The first rule of any technology used in a business is that automation applied to an efficient operation will magnify the efficiency. The second is that automation applied to an inefficient operation will magnify the inefficiency."

Success with Revenue Performance Management does not come from merely investing in technology. It requires that you take part in transforming processes by aligning marketing and sales around a commonly defined revenue process. It requires investing in high quality data that underpins your lead and revenue operations. And that's true regardless of which technology you end up using; how you use this technology will end up mattering much more than what you use. As Lance Armstrong likes to say, "It's not about the bike, it's the rider."

We will now conclude Part III by returning to the human side of the equation, the art of creating revenue.

KEY POINTS

- While it's theoretically possible to manage marketing leads and programs manually, the Internet-driven acceleration and the volume of lead data require help from automation.

- Consistently applying these processes across departments, and effectively analyzing marketing-related data, both require automation help.

- CRM systems are very helpful in managing prospect contact data, but they do not include end-to-end revenue cycle management tools.

- Marketing Automation (MA) applications not only manage lead information; they also include functions that manage marketing tasks and workflow.

- RPM provides a platform into which many different applications can be connected, integrated, and coordinated.

- An RPM platform is an extended MA system, often integrated with CRM, that includes such features as sales productivity metrics, business process modeling, and revenue analytics.

CHAPTER 21

Never Forget the Creative Side of Revenue Creation

The past six chapters have been all about process, analytics, and technology. But I feel compelled to conclude this part of the book with an important reminder: No amount of technology or business process transformation alone can unlock the full potential for growth that Revenue Performance Management affords. Even a well-executed, high-tech, precision campaign to market an ugly lump of coal will not yield great results.

Leading revenue consultant and author Kristin Zhivago has been widely quoted for her observation that "Marketing has shifted from 80 percent creative and 20 percent logistics to 80 percent logistics and 20 percent creative." That idea has gone viral among thought leaders in the area of marketing and sales, because she has a point. There is no doubt the job of the revenue professional, in both marketing and sales, has changed forever. Digital technologies pervade every aspect of buying today, forcing revenue professionals to adopt advanced technology approaches to the marketing and selling experience as well. They are using those technologies to find, nurture, and prioritize leads, and their impact extends all the way to the salesperson reeling in the live ones.

As a result, board members and senior executives have developed heightened expectations of accountability in marketing budgets, a change that in turn has transformed the CMO's job from one focused on brand and message, to one that must also embrace numbers and quantitative results. Many observers say that among revenue professionals, the left brain—the science/analytics side—has taken over from the right brain, the creative/intuitive/emotional side.

However, I am a contrarian on this topic, and while I respect Ms. Zhivago's point, I think it's overstated. Ever since the Industrial Revolution, we have been conditioned to the idea that science and technology *replace* the arts and crafts culture that came before it. And in lots of areas, such as precision manufacturing, that has indeed been the case. But the world of creating revenue is different. The artistic aspects of marketing and sales remain very much alive. In a world where content is so critically important—where brand, social media, and demand programs all interact in intimate ways—it is the creative, right-brain side of marketing that's truly more important than ever before.

As we noted in the last several chapters, the entire buying process starts with awareness, and as we know, the ability to create awareness falls into the province of branding and advertising. You can measure and model customer behavior with technology and analytics, but "moving" human beings to actually prefer your brand and products requires you to excite their imagination. Buyers live in a noisy world, one in which social media users are able to detect and call out falsehoods, hype, and exaggeration in the blink of an eye. All this has greatly elevated the need to break through the clutter with creative, compelling, truthful content and big ideas. This is the only way to get buyers to listen.

We also know that content that truly engages prospects serves as the bait that makes inbound marketing work. One of the most critical moments in the entire revenue cycle happens when a prospective buyer offers his or her contact information in exchange for something they perceive to be of value. That value typically involves interesting, educational, entertaining, useful, and accessible content in various forms and manifestations of the marketer's art.

With lead nurturing, too, content is king. Marketers that keep in touch with and guide early stage buyers from seed to sale must offer a fresh, ongoing stream of content. That's the only way to maintain the buyers' interest, meet their research and evaluation needs, and stay top-of-mind for that magical moment when the buyer is ready to purchase. In fact, I would argue that the emerging importance of inbound marketing and lead nurturing have made branding and advertising, along with the authoring and design of compelling content, more important than they have ever been in the history of marketing. It's a facet of the marketing art that needs to be produced in greater quantity, and with more real relevance to the buyer, than ever before.

There is also an art to effective selling. Even as we transform sales effectiveness by changing the ways salespeople spend their time, we can't forget the artistic dimension that is just as vital to developing, negotiating, and closing a sale. The best salespeople have an uncanny ability to "read the room"—to sense what a buyer is thinking, identify who is moving forward toward a closed deal, and recognize who is really not interested. Great salespeople work at every step of their process to forge an emotional connection with their prospects. I don't think there's any way to really teach sales pros to know exactly when that magic moment arrives to ask for the deal. It's an art. I would even bet that if you asked them, more salespeople would tell you they see themselves falling into the right-brain camp than you'd find among marketers.

The sophisticated technologies and advanced analytics of Revenue Performance Management really do give revenue professionals an unprecedented ability to excel at their jobs. However, it's the art created by the people doing those jobs that inspires someone even to consider what you are selling in the first place, let alone move them to buy it. By balancing the science of marketing and sales with the essential art of those assignments, successful revenue professionals are able to accelerate predictable, expanding revenue across the revenue cycle.

Celebrated social scientist and media theorist Marshall McLuhan once said: "Advertising is the greatest art form of the twentieth century." Even though we have moved on to a new century—one pervaded by digital media and new marketing technologies—McLuhan's observation still rings true today.

The first three parts of this book have taken stock of the current state of buying, marketing, and selling, and illustrated the profound improvements in revenue efficiency and growth that are available to business leaders who adopt and improve a Revenue Performance Management strategy. We've also covered the specific business processes, analytics, and technologies that these people need to put RPM into action. In the final part of this book, we'll look at people, organizations, and catalysts for change, and we'll lay out a roadmap for putting Revenue Performance Management into action at your company.

KEY POINTS

- The often-cited observation that marketing has transitioned from primarily creative to mainly logistical in nature is insightful, but overstated.

- The creative elements of marketing and sales are even more important today in cutting through the noise of the marketplace and exciting buyer interest.

- A great deal of success in sales involves art, intuition, and instinct that can neither be taught nor replaced by technology.

- Finding the right balance of art and science is the key to success for revenue professionals today.

PART IV

PUTTING THE PIECES TOGETHER

Inciting Your Revenue Revolution

CHAPTER 22

Old Models
Up Against the Wall!

We used to think that revolutions are the cause of
change. Actually it is the other way around: change
prepares the ground for revolution.
—*Eric Hoffer*

Revolution is indeed in the air. The traditional sales and marketing
model that somehow managed to limp by for a century or more is
now hopelessly broken and simply can't cut it in a world where buyers,
not sellers, have emerged in unchallenged control of the revenue generation process. Corporations and business people all over the world
are now waking up to that fact. And the most forward-looking among
them are moving swiftly to disrupt the status quo in their marketing
and sales teams by adopting new strategies, processes, and technologies to transform the ways they create, manage, and accelerate revenue
growth.

Though Hoffer's quote is almost a half-century old, it is strikingly apropos for the current revenue revolution. You see, the necessary change has already taken place. Digital technologies like the
web, search, mobile, and social media have forever transformed
the way people buy everything from inexpensive consumer products to
multimillion-dollar business goods.

This change has prepared the ground for innovative marketing
and sales leaders to dramatically rethink their traditional roles and
processes. Those who do, and then act accordingly, will find more
buyers, increase their marketing and sales efficiency, take share

---

from competitors, and grow their revenue to the collective tune of $2.5 trillion by 2017.

Those who don't will fall behind, and find themselves on the losing side in this revolution.

> A revolution is an idea which has found its bayonets.
> —*Napoleon Bonaparte*

This revenue revolution is not merely a good idea, nor is it simply an academic rethinking of marketing and sales. We have found our bayonet; it is called Revenue Performance Management. And we have described a new strategic blueprint for disruptive revenue growth that is both concrete and actionable.

RPM requires that companies implement specific new business practices to shape the revenue creation process, find and nurture more prospective buyers, and prioritize one-on-one sales time, thereby allowing salespeople to close more revenue, more efficiently. Along with new processes come new metrics, which allow you to measure and forecast revenue creation in ways not previously possible, and which enable a journey of continuous improvement in revenue performance going forward.

> The revolution is not an apple that falls when it is ripe.
> You have to make it drop.
> —*Che Guevara*

Although Revenue Performance Management calls for the implementation of new business processes, it is actually much more than that. Because these new processes cut directly across traditional organizational boundaries in most companies, their implications extend to organizational structure and corporate culture. Some people's cheese will be moved.

Jim Collins, author of the best-selling business book *Good to Great*, wrote something a while back that really stuck with me. He said that the biggest productivity leap you can make in a business is to break down the barriers between its functions. And that is exactly what

Revenue Performance Management does—it breaks down the barriers between sales and marketing. Breaking these walls, once and for all, is so critical because sales controls top-line growth, its efficiency is central to the P&L performance of every business, and because marketing is essential to feed buyers into that sales channel.

So the time is right for a disruptive revolution in the ways businesses create revenue, and we now have a concrete blueprint for transformative action. But change is never easy, especially not when it involves challenging such deeply entrenched—and traditionally divided—parts of the corporation. As we discussed in Chapter 5, Marketing is from Venus and Sales is from Mars. They really are different organizations, with different skills and different cultures.

However, there's a distinction between evolution and revolution. Business leaders who opt to wait for a revolutionary change to occur organically between marketing and sales will be waiting a long time, and waiting for something to happen is a proven recipe for losing out in business revolutions. But before you start to think that inciting this kind of revolution is a bridge too far, especially given the inertia of the modern corporation, remember: It has been done before. Six Sigma, for example, revolutionized manufacturing and quality processes, and Agile Development totally revolutionized product development. Sales and marketing are not doomed to speak in different languages and to work at cross-purposes for eternity.

In earlier chapters, I described this book as a manifesto for Revenue Performance Management. Now I have made the call for a disruptive revenue revolution built into this manifesto's tenets. This fourth and final section of *Revenue Disruption* will therefore offer some ideas about steps you can take to make the apple drop for your own revenue revolution. The blueprint looks something like this:

- Realize that revenue creation starts when a company first meets a prospective buyer and continues to close a deal, and beyond. Accordingly, marketing and sales have no choice but to collaborate at every step of a joint revenue cycle.

- Manage the marketing department as a true revenue-generating organization. Set objectives and incentives for marketing leaders in line with this charter.

- Implement a systematic process by which you move prospective buyers forward through the revenue cycle, and measure their engagement at every step.

- Provide sales teams with the information and tools they need to prioritize their time so they can engage with the most qualified prospective buyers at exactly the moment each is ready to act.

- Measure the effectiveness and ROI of spending on people and programs at every step of the revenue cycle, across both marketing and sales. Continuously adjust them to improve the processes based on these measurements.

- Evolve the organization of marketing and sales toward a single, unified team responsible for revenue creation and growth.

CHAPTER 23

The First Steps on Your RPM Journey

I t's a bit perverse to put it this way, but one piece of good news about implementing Revenue Performance Management is that there's so much waste and inefficiency in most marketing and sales organizations that a new RPM initiative can pay for itself very quickly. There's plenty of low hanging fruit in most companies to go after in the early days, and having quick successes is valuable because it reinforces organizational commitment and confidence. But, as I have tried to make clear throughout this book, implementing a Revenue Performance Management strategy is a *journey*. It is a long-term commitment to systematic business transformation—one that touches processes, organization structures, information technologies, and metrics. It is also a journey of continuous improvement, in which ongoing monitoring and measurement is fed back into increasingly efficient revenue generation and growth.

There's a familiar adage that goes, "The hardest part of any journey is taking the first step," and it certainly applies here. Because RPM directly affects so many deeply entrenched elements of a company's organization and culture, including changes in people's job descriptions, the journey's beginning can seem scary and may often encounter resistance. In this chapter, we'll explore some of the first steps leaders can take to get under way with a Revenue Performance Management journey of their own. I hope that a nugget or two of this advice will make it a bit easier to get going.

There are numerous aspects of a successful RPM launch, all of which are intertwined, including leadership, organizational alignment, technology, and initial project scope. Since nothing happens without leadership, that's a good place to start.

RPM AS A CEO IMPERATIVE

Consider this: Even though many publicly traded companies have been reporting strong earnings, and parts of the economy have recovered from the depths of the recession that began in 2008, their performance hasn't always translated into higher stock values. Because these strong earnings often came by way of staff cuts and other cost reductions, real growth has been scarce. As a result, Wall Street has increasingly turned its attention toward the top line, demanding to see more progress on revenue performance.

That's not news to CEOs or other senior business leaders. For the past three years, revenue growth has been their main objective, according to Frost & Sullivan's annual CEO Survey. But what's interesting is to observe how CEOs think about accomplishing it: The largest proportion cites *increasing sales* as their number one strategy for achieving their growth goals.

This survey result caught my attention because while increasing sales is a hugely important *goal*, it is not a strategy in and of itself. It's a little bit like saying that one's strategy for losing twenty pounds is to "drop a few pounds every week." It says nothing about *how* you're actually planning to accomplish it. So the real question for these CEOs is this: What is your strategy for increasing sales? And how do you plan to actually accomplish that growth goal?

The responding CEOs in the Frost & Sullivan survey identified myriad textbook strategies to achieve their growth goals, including strategic partnerships, customer strategies, new product development, and expansion into new markets. But something critical was missing: a focus on improving the company's sales and marketing effectiveness as a way to increase revenue performance. Perhaps that's why this same group of CEOs also indicated that they have less than full confidence in their organizations' ability to conduct core growth strategies; it's as though more of the same simply didn't inspire much confidence.

Of course, I think that Revenue Performance Management answers the question of how to achieve fundamental growth. And because it's clear that any growth agenda starts in the CEO's office, RPM is a strategy that must originate there as well. I have a vision, and it goes like this: Pretty soon, every CEO will turn to his or her team, and ask, "What are we doing about Revenue Performance Management?"

A transition to Revenue Performance Management has significant implications for a company's internal operations over time. As marketing generates more good leads, and therefore increases sales efficiency, investments in the marketing department will also tend to increase. Those will be offset by savings captured from the increased sales efficiency. As marketing leaders and staff become more directly accountable for revenue, their compensation structures will tend to become more leveraged and look more like traditional sales comp plans. As a maturing, end-to-end Revenue Cycle Model yields new metrics and increases long-range revenue forecast accuracy, corporate dashboards will evolve, and managers will need to interpret this new data as a guide to future actions.

All of this suggests that the entire senior leadership team in a company or operating division needs to be on the same page about RPM. The CFO must be ready and willing to implement the shifts and changes that RPM entails. Sales and marketing executives need to form a new alliance. And others, like manufacturing executives, need to take cues from new and important metrics.

In January of 1996, Jack Welch publicly announced the launch of a Six Sigma initiative at General Electric. He had developed a passion for the topic and committed his personal leadership to it. He built GE's program to drive Six Sigma. He gave the initiative a name and identity. He set clear and measurable goals. He changed compensation and incentive structures. And he implemented new standards for promotion tied to Six Sigma. In short, he took all the steps needed to let everyone inside and outside GE know just how serious he was about this new initiative.

Executive leaders should look closely at how Welch catalyzed this transformation at GE, and they should consider applying similar strategies to weave RPM into their own corporate fabric.

CREATING "TEAM REVENUE" WITHIN THE CORPORATION

The top sales executive at a prominent technology company, who was himself an early adopter of RPM, recently described the marketing and sales relationship at many of the companies he had encountered. "It's a lot like a dysfunctional marriage," he said. "The husband and wife have forgotten why they got married in the first place, what made them such a great couple, a team. Those of us in marketing and sales must remember that we too are also members of the same team. And just like the couples in successful, long-lasting marriages, we need to approach business challenges and opportunities together, leveraging our collaborative strengths."

The sales executive continued: "It doesn't really matter if the fault lies with marketing or sales, or even both. There are two sides to every coin, and at least two versions of every problem. Pointing fingers and saying things like, 'marketing couldn't deliver quality leads,' or 'sales couldn't close them,' does no one any good. The only thing that matters is achieving revenue growth, and that requires us to come together as an integrated operation to solve problems and work the revenue cycle in a coordinated way. That's what it takes to create a high output, revenue-centric organization. Ultimately, that's what RPM is all about."

The best marketing leaders see the world in much the same way. Susanne Lyons, the former CMO of Visa USA and Charles Schwab & Co., has been on the front lines of helping to catalyze these changes in the corporate revenue process. She recently told me how the sales culture has become less "individual-driven," as it moves toward more of a revenue-centric ecosystem within the corporation.

"What's really interesting is how companies are now using advanced data mining and sophisticated marketing automation tools to enable both the marketing and sales organizations to do continuous improvement, share best practices, and drive better results," Susanne said. "Through these new technologies and processes, we are seeing sales and marketing collaborate on refining messaging and learning organically from each other. This would not have been possible without the new RPM tools and processes that more and more corporations throughout the United States and around the world are embracing."

Susanne continued: "It's no longer just the lone star sales guy, hiding all of his sales secrets. The best companies are figuring out what's working and then finding efficient ways to quickly share those strategies and best practices across the entire organization. They then continue to refine and improve those practices, throwing out what isn't working and constantly refining and improving what is. As part of a continuously improving cycle and loop, this process helps to drive greater productivity, increased sales, and more revenue. More than anything, this process improvement approach is a huge part of the power and promise of RPM."

It's a beautiful thing when an experienced sales executive, and an equally experienced marketing executive, can articulate with such clarity and consistency what it takes to build an integrated revenue leadership process spanning marketing and sales. One team, one integrated process, and one objective: revenue growth.

Of course, it may take a bit of nudging from the CEO and other senior leaders to get marketing and sales pointed in the same direction, particularly in organizations where this degree of clarity and consistency is not so evident. Obviously, when a CEO makes an organization's priorities clear (as Jack Welch did with Six Sigma) other executives tend to line up and salute. But a few more management techniques can reinforce the message.

The senior revenue leader in the company, whether it's the CEO, COO, President, or other senior general manager, needs to appoint a team explicitly charged with governing the RPM initiative. This will consist of senior sales and marketing executives themselves, or high-level designates on their teams with operational responsibility. Companies must organize this team as one consisting of peers, with neither marketing nor sales in charge of the initiative. And all members should be held responsible to speak in one voice about plans and measurements.

With few exceptions, no one ever taught revenue leaders about the ins and outs of RPM; it's something they'll need to invest the time to learn and the effort to understand. If they haven't already read this book, or one like it, then they'll need to.

Finally, all successful revenue leaders are motivated by incentives, and some incentives can help to get the ball rolling. The incentive for sales is pretty clear: If marketing is able to deliver a steady stream of well-qualified leads, sales efficiency and quota attainment will go up. That's a fundamental equation of RPM, after all. Because this increase in attainment comes from true efficiency gains, sales leaders need to hear a commitment from senior management that their quotas won't just rise in line with sales growth, but that they will personally share— financially, that is—in the company's improved revenue and efficiency.

The incentive should be only slightly less pecuniary for marketing. After all, the best marketing leaders have long yearned for a "seat at the revenue table." They need a commitment to attend the revenue call and to have a voice in forecasting future revenue, and a compensation structure for themselves and their staff that shares the rewards of upside revenue performance with the team responsible for creating so many of those qualified sales leads.

YES, YOU GOTTA BUY SOME SOFTWARE

If there's one thing that has characterized my own leadership style over the past 30 years, it's that I'm a very direct guy. I tend not to sugarcoat things; I call 'em as I see 'em. So even though I may feel a twinge of guilt because I appear to be self-serving by advocating a software purchase that could benefit my company, I want to make a blunt point: Revenue Performance Management *does need* a software platform. If you're going to embark on this journey, you will need to purchase and roll out the tools to make it work and to measure its success. So a necessary early action item for your RPM leadership team is to begin the evaluation and purchase of an RPM software system.

In Chapter 20, we looked at the reasons why RPM needs a software platform to work effectively. We also reviewed some key features and functions the software provides, so I won't repeat those points here.

The good news is that the RPM systems today are one of the most competitive and innovative segments of the entire business software universe. There are a number of excellent options among which you can choose. This is true for the world's largest corporations, for small businesses, for budding start-ups, and for every company in between.

And there is even better news: An RPM purchase can quickly become a very high-return investment. As I mentioned at the start of this chapter, there's a lot of low hanging fruit available. I have had new users of RPM systems tell me they were able to pay for their entire investment solely out of improved conversions from inbound marketing activities like Google advertising. With their RPM system now paid for, the strategic revenue performance improvements that result from increased sales productivity are all gravy.

Finally, I should note that there is a wealth of buying advice available for anyone considering an investment in an RPM system. Analysts at leading IT research firms like Gartner, Forrester Research, IDC, and SiriusDecisions pay close attention to the emerging RPM technology market. They can provide independent advice to prospective buyers. And, not surprisingly, most RPM software vendors have mastered the use of inbound marketing—seed nurturing—in their own companies. So if you type "revenue performance management" or "marketing automation" into Google, or ask your friends on Facebook or LinkedIn, you'll learn everything you need to know about taking control of your own RPM buying process.

SELECTING AN INITIAL PROJECT SCOPE

Since every company is different, every RPM initiative will be unique. The key is to take that first hard step on the journey—to get yourself going.

In a small company with just a couple of sales reps, or a new company just beginning to sell, the scope of an initial RPM project can be quite simple. Everyone in marketing and sales participates, and management attention should immediately focus on the creation of great content, basic lead nurturing and scoring processes, and getting more well-qualified leads into the hands of sales.

However, it can be more daunting to get started in a larger, more mature company. Where do you begin?

First of all, many larger companies have multiple divisions, product lines, sales teams, and geographies in which sales take place. There are also multiple routes to market including channels, partners, and direct sales forces. So just pick one to start. You can base this decision on guidelines such as: Which marketing team has the ability to produce compelling content to feed the needs of inbound marketing and lead nurturing? What group has a marketing leader with proven skills in thinking about processes and metrics? Where is there a sales leader with a high degree of curiosity and receptivity to change?

Second, take inventory—literally. Most mature companies have existing databases of leads that they've gathered from various marketing programs that they've run in the past. And many mature companies have SFA or CRM systems that are groaning under the weight of dormant leads or sales opportunities. These lead pools can be great assets to get RPM moving. The entire RPM initiative can achieve a quick win if a lead nurturing process can activate a few dormant leads from a marketing database or CRM system. So start where there's already a pool of leads to prime the pump.

CREATING A NEW NARRATIVE FOR CHANGE

We have seen that by making critical changes, across the entire revenue process, companies can balance their marketing and sales investments more effectively than ever. They leverage large-scale changes in buyer behavior to find, nurture, qualify, and deliver more sales-ready leads to their front-line sales people, and they align marketing and sales organizations into a single, revenue-focused team.

Together, these steps can unlock new revenue efficiencies and translate them into real top-line growth. Then lather, rinse, and repeat. Analyze early wins, and celebrate them to reinforce the organization's commitment to RPM. Over the longer term, your Revenue Performance Management journey can completely transform the way your company creates—thereby changing the arc of your business completely.

This simple narrative needs to become the mantra of your senior leaders, RPM project sponsors, and the entire revenue team. Teach it. Repeat it. Create a shared vision. And reap the rewards.

KEY POINTS

- There is a lot of low-hanging fruit in the search for improved marketing and sales efficiency, so the payback for an RPM initiative can be very fast.

- Executive leadership is critical to RPM success, and many CEOs say they want increased sales to satisfy investors. However, they usually lack a focus on improving their marketing and sales functions.

- RPM requires executive leadership to champion changes in the structure, tasks, and compensation plans of the company's marketing and sales personnel.

- High quality software systems are currently available to enable RPM implementation, and expert consultation from major IT research firms is also available to advise clients.

- Every company needs to find its own first step in initiating an RPM business process.

CHAPTER 24

To Win the Revenue Game, You Need a Playbook

I t's fine to talk about marketing and sales alignment in the abstract. After all, it's one of the key success factors in building an RPM strategy. But it's a whole lot better seeing how these ideas are put into action.

My favorite part in writing this book was having the opportunity to share ideas with some of the best thinkers and most astute innovators in marketing and sales. Some are corporate executives who truly understand the massive changes that are currently transforming the ways corporations create, manage, and accelerate revenue. They are also people who have helped lead the way to implementing Revenue Performance Management at their own companies.

One of those individuals is Wes Wasson, the Senior Vice President and Chief Marketing Officer of Citrix Systems, an industry leader in mobile workstyles and cloud computing, and one of the world's top five SaaS software vendors. Wes has more than 20 years of experience in technology marketing. Prior to Citrix, Wes held senior marketing leadership positions at Sun Microsystems, where he helped the company achieve number one market positions across several key segments, and Network Associates, where he contributed to their growth from a small single-product company into a $1 billion industry leader.

DRIVING REVENUE PERFORMANCE WITH A COMMON PLAYBOOK

During our interview, Wes discussed a powerful idea he had instituted at Citrix to ensure strong alignment and tight integration between the company's global marketing and sales departments. The idea was to create a single "playbook" that both the marketing and sales teams could use to formulate joint strategies, guide their activities, and drive increased revenue at Citrix.

Here are some excerpts from my interview with Wes about the marketing/sales playbook he has been using so effectively at Citrix.

Phil Fernandez: Wes, what was the genesis of your playbook idea?

Wes Wasson: My core philosophy from early on has been to think of sales and marketing in the context of a single demand chain, an integrated process. It starts with a belief that this really is a single chain. So, in thinking about the recipe for success with this integrated approach—and this was long before technology innovations started really changing things in our profession—the key was to have a common way to measure sales and marketing success. What that means is that success on the front end of the chain is a hundred percent irrelevant if the end of the chain doesn't deliver the finished product.

Think of a scenario like this: The marketing team at the front end of a bottling plant is celebrating and cheering and giving high-fives because it exceeded its quota in creating bottle caps and labels. Meanwhile, gallons of beer have been spilling onto the middle of the floor, so the salespeople at the end of the production line aren't able to deliver what they need. If there isn't a common, agreed-to measure of success from one end of the line to the other, there won't be any results that actually matter. Making sure we always have these joint goals and metrics between sales and marketing was the catalyst for creating our common playbook.

PF: One example of the dysfunction that I cite in this book is the fact that sales and marketing can't even agree on something as fundamental as the definition of a sales-ready lead. How did you address that at Citrix?

WW: That's actually one of the areas we're constantly refining. Certainly, the innovations from Revenue Performance Management vendors are helping to solve this long-running problem. Powerful new revenue management technologies have given us the ability to very quickly assess and measure the elements that go into a sales-ready lead. We're now able to take a lead to opportunity, and actually close the deal cycle, while measuring the conversion rates and lead velocity through the entire revenue cycle funnel. We also know where any bottlenecks are by region, product, and campaign. Even in the relatively recent past, this kind of revenue cycle visibility was virtually impossible. By helping us better define and pinpoint critical steps in the revenue process, like sales-ready leads, these new innovations are empowering marketing and salespeople to work more effectively together to improve overall results.

PF: So tell us how you developed the playbook.

WW: The first thing I did was to have my VP of demand marketing effectively become a member of the sales team, which is led by my colleague, Senior VP of Sales and Services, Al Monserrat. My head of demand marketing still reported to me, and I still had control of a centralized marketing budget, but he was as much a part of Al's sales organization as he was of my marketing group. At the same time, we realized that we needed to align our strategies and plans to ensure that my team's marketing activities and Al's sales efforts were working in concert to achieve shared goals. That's when we realized that we needed to create a common "playbook" according to which both marketing and sales would operate.

The playbook's real power is that it makes everything very transparent. It has built-in checks and balances that totally changed the equation for us. And that led to a big increase in trust between marketing and sales. As a result, the quality of the marketing increased substantially, and so did its impact on ROI.

PF: What made the playbook such an important part of achieving these improved results?

WW: The idea for a common marketing/sales playbook is gaining currency in business because of the traditional disconnects between marketing and sales. It is hard to achieve your overall corporate goals, which are ultimately growth and profitability, when marketing and sales use such different metrics for success. Sales measures success principally by revenue, while demand marketing metrics typically track things like lead development and conversions. The playbook is incredibly important because it helps us to harmonize these measurement disconnects by providing a common basis for understanding and measuring the activities and outcomes for both marketing and sales. Creating a common go-to-market playbook can also provide tremendous clarity of focus companywide. When product groups, support, supply chain, finance, and operations know exactly where the revenue side of the business is focused, it becomes far easier to align everyone's contribution to revenue.

PF: What is the playbook's actual structure?

WW: At the beginning of each year, Al and I gather our teams together to do some formal planning and figure out the six to eight key "plays" that will make up that year's playbook. This is very much a collaborative process. For each play, we define the opportunity, an identifiable buyer, an identifiable offer, and the value proposition. The key is to make each play repeatable. Some are more strategic, while others are more tactical and short-cycle, but all are expressed as a complete solution to a common customer problem.

Once Al and I have signed off on our common playbook, I can then stand up at his sales kick-off meetings and say, "This is exactly what we're planning to do this year. We are going to create demand for these six things—period. Nothing else." The process really works because Al and his senior sales leaders also have ownership of the playbook. Their plans, forecasts, and training programs are all designed around the same playbook. As a result, we all end up working from a common game plan.

The Citrix playbooks, and the process that Wes Wasson and Al Monserrat use to create them, offer a valuable lesson to all revenue professionals. They required trust to build a true cross-functional team to develop the playbooks, and a shared leadership vision to align their entire organizations to execute them in an end-to-end process. Every marketing and sales leader should consider a similar process in the early days of his or her RPM journey.

KEY POINTS

- The Citrix philosophy views marketing and sales as component parts of a single demand chain that requires common metrics.

- At Citrix, sales and marketing jointly develop playbooks at the start of each year featuring six to eight key plays; both groups then have ownership of the resulting plans.

- Revenue Performance Management software helps Citrix to assess the elements that constitute a sales-ready lead and provide transparency into potential problems.

- Assigning a senior marketing person to participate in sales meetings helps to better align their strategies and plans.

CHAPTER 25

Should You Appoint a Chief Revenue Officer?

A primary theme running throughout this entire book has been the need for marketing and sales alignment. This requires that companies create processes that seamlessly span both departments—for example, those that involve lead nurturing, scoring, and recycling. It also means that organizations must team up for other go-to-market activities, as epitomized by the Citrix Systems playbooks described in the previous chapter. But even more important than joint processes and programs are the ways executive sales leaders and their marketing counterparts create personal alliances based on a shared vision of Revenue Performance Management.

In truth, there's something awkward about this whole construct. I have been struck while writing this book by the number of times I've had to use a phrase about how "marketing and sales leaders" need to come together to agree to a plan, review a joint metric, or otherwise coordinate their activities. Of course, cross-functional collaboration is essential to any well-performing business. So on the surface, it may not be surprising that I've repeatedly emphasized this need for cooperation.

However, when you dig a little deeper, you start to see that this whole idea is fundamentally off track and simply not sustainable. In a world where the buyer is in control, and where the adoption of Revenue Performance Management strategies has begun to result in seamless processes that flow back and forth between marketing and sales, the two organizations need to be more than just close partners. Ultimately, they need to come together into one integral revenue machine.

Make no mistake. I am not suggesting that salespeople should become marketers, or vice versa. There are many different jobs and roles that need to be performed across the revenue cycle. And as we've seen, different revenue jobs attract different personality types. Lots of departments in modern corporations have people performing very different jobs such as accounts payable clerks, revenue analysts, IT specialists, and HR professionals, all of whom often coexist quite successfully within one G&A organization led by the CFO. But it often makes sense to put all of these functions together under one leader, because they all share a joint mission of supporting the company's people and business operations.

Okay, okay, I know what you're thinking. This idea could really mess with some people's cheese. Cats sleeping with dogs! Pick your favorite metaphor. But today's marketing and sales professionals really are part of the same team that shares a single mission: To enhance revenue, profit, and growth. They are integral participants in one unified business process called Revenue Performance Management. So when you think about it that way, it makes neither strategic nor operational sense to have separate executives managing sales and marketing. It's time we got on with reinventing the corporate organization chart, and we can start by erasing the artificial line between marketing and sales.

But who should run this new revenue organization? My answer is that virtually every company should appoint a Chief Revenue Officer, or CRO. This is a new C-level executive who is responsible for all aspects of a corporation's revenue performance, from the way it meets new prospective buyers, through creating awareness, conducting awesome web and social marketing, nurturing leads, right on to reeling in the live ones, and then beyond—to managing the full revenue life cycle of customer retention and renewals.

Note that the CRO is not simply an expanded role for the CMO, VP of sales, or VP of marketing. Rather, this individual's job is to be the company's *revenue architect*. As such, he or she must create strategies for growth; catalyze the design of the revenue cycle; implement the processes that support it; and drive the organization's commitment to continuous measurement and improvement. That same individual must also identify ways to organize marketing and sales professionals into new and innovative team structures that respond to the realities of modern buying; establish compensation schemes that instill equitable incentives across all members of the revenue team; allocate and dynamically manage investments across each step in the revenue cycle to maximize efficiency and effectiveness; and be a inspirational cheerleader for revenue results.

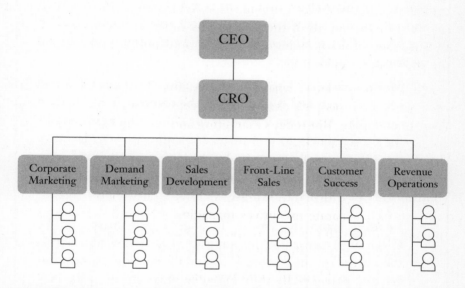

FIGURE 25.1 The Chief Revenue Officer, or CRO, is a single corporate executive officer responsible for marketing and sales. The CRO does not just oversee two separate departments, but is responsible for managing them as one seamless organization.

The CRO must assume a long-term, integrated perspective, rather than the short-term horizon that sales departments usually embrace. At the same time, the CRO must have a passion for driving deals and quarterly revenue results in balance with the marketing team's longer-term programs and more meticulously planned work styles. The best CROs understand and embrace the differences between marketing and sales, while at the same time establishing processes to ensure their coordination across the full revenue cycle.

OTHER VOICES AND VIEWS ON THE ROLE
OF CHIEF REVENUE OFFICER

I've talked to a number of executives about the role of the Chief
Revenue Officer over the past several years. Some carried the
title CRO themselves, others managed people with that title,
and others still aspired to earn a CRO role at some point in
the future. I'd like to share a few insightful comments I found
inspiring about this role:

- **Market maker:** "The CRO works closely with the CEO and
  others to craft and communicate the company's vision, then
  turns that vision into a strategy for pioneering new markets
  for the company to dominate. He knows how to leverage
  this effort into short-term objectives that result in category
  creation, brand expansion, product positioning, packaging,
  buyer awareness, lead creation, and sales excellence."

- **Leading from the front**: "Business is a team sport. The
  CRO must see and communicate a shared vision across
  the entire revenue process, including employees, customers, and partners. By thinking a few steps ahead of the current business, he or she inspires the revenue team as well
  as the entire company. This person must be balanced and
  competitive—in a team sports way—someone who expects
  to win every time. CROs think at a strategic level, but 'get
  their jollies' by making deals happen. He or she is able to
  assess complex situations with great insight, and then communicate what the team should do to remain focused on the
  right measurable goals."

- **Business acumen**: "The Chief Revenue Officer is a business leader first, a 'sales and marketing person' second. She
  understands the business model. She works closely with the
  CFO and CEO to determine budget trade-offs with a goal
  of continually improving results across sales, marketing,
  renewal, and product teams. She's the person with whom the

CFO and CEO meet to discuss strategic and tactical decisions across customer success, renewals, demand/pipeline generation, product roadmap, partners, market positioning, competition, and sales processes. She's someone who other C-level execs can trust to step in for the CEO and CFO if a tactical or strategic challenge arises while the other C-level execs are at work on different priorities."

- **Data/metrics-driven**: "The CRO must have an intense focus on concrete details to keep the company real. He creates a culture of accountability across sales and marketing by setting the right metrics and tying compensation and promotions to real results, not just to emotions. The CRO needs to identify and fix issues across the revenue teams immediately, before the situation becomes dire and more costly to the company's success. Success and failure belong to the entire revenue team, not just to sales or marketing. The CRO must personally feel and effectively communicate his own accountability for the company's success; by sharing that conviction, he raises expectations of a similar commitment from his people."

- **Wise arbiter**: "The CRO makes the right trade-offs across sales and marketing in order to continually improve productivity across all teams. He will naturally think about investing deeper in fewer initiatives versus investing in new initiatives."

- **Focused on results**: "The Chief Revenue Officer has to have a successful track record of owning and growing bookings. She should be able to commit to short-term results, forecast future revenue, and take accountability for both short-term success and longer-term strategic value. The CRO is driven to capture all viable leads, and to win every 'good' sales deal. To do this, the CRO prioritizes investments and time on the most likely buyers, then implements processes and systems to ensure scaling and forecasting across the entire revenue funnel."

HIRING A CRO FOR ALL THE RIGHT REASONS

The role of Chief Revenue Officer seems to be gaining momentum, and I have recently noticed more and more corporations naming CROs. And from what I can tell, they are doing so for varying reasons—some very good, some probably not so much.

However, one must always implement the CRO structure strategically. Revenue Performance Management requires profound shifts in the way companies manage their sales and marketing functions. Appointing a CRO to be the instigator and steward of this transformation is the right reason for doing so, and many of the best companies are getting this exactly right.

Yet I have seen too many other cases where the CRO title is used simply as a perk and promotion, a highfalutin new title for the same old job. It's dangerous to generalize too much, but it often seems that the title is given as a promotion to the VP of sales, perhaps to create C-level parity with the Chief Marketing Officer. That's a mistake. The CRO's mission needs to be one of binding marketing and sales into a single team, not of "keeping up with the Joneses."

But is CRO really a new job? What about the title of President, or Chief Operating Officer? In many companies, one or both of these titles is held by the executive who manages both marketing and sales. So doesn't that mean companies really have had Chief Revenue Officers for years, only with a different, more traditional name? Maybe, but only rarely, as far as I can tell. In most cases, the person in this role might manage both marketing and sales, but they are not thinking every day about a unified revenue architecture. They do not feel free to seamlessly allocate and reallocate resources between marketing and sales, and they are not leading a transformative organizational change. Such a person may be a perfectly capable leader, but he or she is not truly a Chief Revenue Officer.

If structured properly and outfitted with the right talent and objectives, the CRO can play a pivotal role in driving revenue growth. That individual becomes both the catalyst for the corporation's Revenue Performance Management initiative and the steward of its success. As a visionary revenue architect who is accountable for driving better integration and alignment between all revenue-related functions, the CRO can become the true leader of an authentic revenue revolution.

KEY POINTS

- Companies can achieve closer collaboration of marketing and sales throughout the revenue cycle by integrating them under a single C-level executive.

- Combining different disciplines and personality types into one corporate function is routine in many areas of business; revenue generation is an obvious candidate.

- A Chief Revenue Officer who is responsible for all aspects of the corporation's revenue performance would serve as the company's primary revenue architect.

- Companies must implement a CRO structure strategically, and not do it simply as a perk or promotion for someone in sales who is doing the same job as before.

- A CRO's responsibilities and focus are not the same as a corporate President or COO; instead, his or her job is to lead the company's Revenue Performance Management initiative.

CHAPTER 26

The Roadmap for Your RPM Journey

For a decade or more, I have had a mantra that has guided my personal approach to leadership. It goes like this:

Think Big, Start Small, Move Quickly

What it means is that you have to dream big, work from a vision, and set audacious goals for yourself and your company. But since the big ideas part can be daunting, it's essential to prevent fear or uncertainty from blocking your way. A journey is just a series of small steps. While not every step needs to move in the direction of your end goal, if enough of them do, you'll get where you want to go.

Finally, run, don't walk. The world is moving faster every year and every day. If you're not acting with urgency in everything you do, you become a sitting duck, just waiting to be crushed by a more aggressive competitor who is running while you are walking.

I can't think of a better place to apply this mantra than to the Revenue Performance Management journey. We have the motivation: Buying has changed forever. We have the vision: Transform the arts and crafts of standalone marketing and sales departments into a unified, high-performance revenue machine. We have the audacious goal: Achieving unprecedented revenue growth, together with increased revenue efficiency, to the tune of $2.5 trillion across the global economy by 2017. We have the strategy: Revenue Performance Management, which is real and achievable, offering an immediate and concrete plan for action. And we have the leader: a Chief Revenue Officer who can lead, inspire, and shepherd this disruptive transformation to fruition.

So here's a roadmap to help you think big, start small, and move quickly with Revenue Performance Management.

- *Reignite Growth: It's the Global Business Imperative.* Growth is the number-one challenge facing corporations and their management teams worldwide. It is certainly the key priority for most of the C-level business executives with whom I regularly speak. Companies simply cannot continue to improve their earnings by cutting people and slashing expenses. What's required is growth—more of it, and with continuously improving profitability.

- *Commit to Transformational Change.* This book is about disruptive transformation. It is not about reorganization, or a new software system, or a project for some middle manager to undertake. Companies today must therefore undertake a fundamental change in the way they create, manage, and accelerate revenue. The fact is that the current sales and marketing models are at best obsolete, at worst totally dysfunctional. The old *Mad Men* approach to generating revenue does not merely need tinkering; it needs to be replaced with a newer, more efficient, more powerful model based on RPM.

- *Adapt or Fail.* As I tried to explain in Chapter 1: It's the buyer, stupid. The shift in power from seller to buyer has already taken place, and the pace of further change is accelerating. Adapting to this reality is not an option for companies who seek to survive and thrive; it's mandatory. Top performing companies will use these powerful new tools, processes, and methodologies to more effectively help buyers find them, and to seamlessly guide early-stage prospects all the way to revenue.

- *Invest in People.* I have talked about building a high-performance revenue machine at a number of points in this book. But I hope I made clear at the same time that this is not a transformation away from people. Human skills—like building a persuasive brand, writing compelling content, and demonstrating true sales savvy—remain just as important, perhaps even more so, in a transformed revenue world. Successful organizations also focus on ways to inspire and develop their best people with the promise of the RPM journey.

- *Pick Your Spot and Move.* One of the best parts about RPM is that there is so much low-hanging fruit to harvest—based on the waste and inefficiency in traditional marketing and sales models—that companies can achieve success, payback, and positive reinforcement quickly and clearly. Not every marketing program or sales team has to change on day one. Simply find a place to start, identify a promising team, pick a motivated leader, and then go.

- *Seek a Small Win First.* It's hard to overstate what a major victory it is when a marketing team and a sales team start to establish a common vocabulary and metrics. Just having the two actually agree on the definition of a sales-ready lead is really pretty momentous. Even a small step like that can begin to transform a revenue organization by allowing marketing people who work further up the revenue funnel to realign their efforts around the common definition. One good sales lead— and one salesperson saying words to the effect of, "Wow, marketing really helped me make my quota"—may be all an RPM transformation needs to take root.

- *Continuously Measure and Improve.* This transformation is never done. A revenue-optimized corporation needs to constantly measure and improve every aspect of its RPM engine. Measuring the effectiveness of the people and programs throughout the entire revenue cycle helps to make sure you can provide predictable results and prove sustained ROI. A high-performing RPM machine is not a "set it and forget it" proposition.

My urgent call to action is this: Join the Revenue Performance Management revolution right now. Break through the last frontier of outdated and underperforming business processes, and fundamentally transform the way your corporation creates, manages, and accelerates its revenue.

KEY POINTS

- "Think big, start small, move quickly" is a mantra that fits the circumstances of most companies contemplating an RPM initiative.

- Guiding principles that can serve as the basis of a blueprint for implementing RPM would include: reigniting growth, committing to transformational change, adapting to a reordered buyer-seller relationship, investing in people, finding a place to start, and seeking a first small win, followed by continuous measurement and improvement.

CHAPTER 27

Viva la Revolution!

There's been a lot of speculation on when I will
deliver a vision. The last thing IBM needs right now is
a vision. What it needs right now are tough-minded,
market-driven, highly effective strategies.
—*Lou Gerstner, 1993*

That was Lou Gerstner, famously responding to a reporter's
question after he took over as IBM's CEO in 1993. Of course,
Gerstner actually did have a pretty big vision in mind for his new
company, one on which he delivered masterfully by reinventing IBM
around software and global services. According to many, Gerstner
saved the storied technology company in the process; IBM had been
declining for years because of its heavy reliance on old technologies
and even older thinking.

To accomplish big, revolutionary things in business, as elsewhere
in life, you need to start with a vision. Having a clear, strong, and compelling picture of what you want to be and where you intend to go
significantly improves your chances of getting there. But having a big
vision is not the enemy of having tough-minded, market-driven, highly
effective strategies.

My vision for this book was always to disrupt the status quo in
terms of how companies create revenue, and to foster a new kind of
corporate structure that would drive outsized growth and success
for businesses worldwide. In this vision, the old dysfunctional sales
and marketing model has been forever replaced by highly efficient

and effective Revenue Performance Management strategies, processes, technologies, and people.

THE POWER AND PROMISE OF REVOLUTIONARY CHANGE

Change happens when great insight combines with audacious action. Fred Smith had a critical insight: that the information revolution would reinvent the global supply chain. That was the genesis of Federal Express. More recently, Mark Zuckerberg had the insight that people are fundamentally social animals who love to share stuff with friends, acquaintances, and colleagues. Thus, Facebook was born. Smith and Zuckerberg got the recipe right, and that caused a lot of light bulbs to click on and ignite waves of global change.

I think this is exactly what we are starting to see with Revenue Performance Management. The bulbs are switching on all over the planet, from Dublin to Detroit, from San Jose to Shanghai. They are finally starting to illuminate the dark corners of ineffective sales and marketing practice that, for too long, have been denied the bright light of change and progress. All of this represents an historic opportunity for the companies and executives with the courage to change, the foresight to lead, and the skill to bring it all together.

More than anything, I hope this book inspires and empowers you to summon the courage to change, the inspiration to lead, and the knowledge necessary to put a big vision into immediate action. By taking that first step, by disrupting the status quo in marketing and sales, by saying goodbye to the dysfunctional relationship that has long characterized their relationship, and embarking on a transformative journey based on Revenue Performance Management, you have the opportunity to incite a Revenue Revolution at your own company—and for yourself.

Marketing and Sales: Welcome to the future. We're glad you made it.

BIBLIOGRAPHY

INTRODUCTION

Knowles, Graeme, "A Conceptual Model for the Application of Six Sigma Methodologies to Supply Chain Improvement." *International Journal of Logistics: Research and Applications* 8, no. 1 (March 2005): 51–65.

Character LLC, "The Maytag Repairman," *Characterweb.com*, 2002, www.characterweb.com/maytag.html.

CHAPTER 1

Donnelly, Tim, "How to Qualify a Sales Lead," *Inc.com*, August 19, 2011, www.inc.com/guides/201108/how-to-qualify-a-sales-lead.html.

Kuper, Simon, "The End of Identity Politics." *FT Magazine*, November 11, 2011, www.ft.com/intl/cms/s/2/0c3bd918-0a5c-11e1-85ca-00144feabdc0.html#axzz1hloxGg4N

Local Automotive Dealerships, "The Role of Interactive Media in the Consumer Car Shopping Process," Yahoo! Search Marketing, January 23, 2012, www.slideshare.net/AutomotiveSocial/the-role-of-interactive-media-in-the-consumer-car-shopping-process.

CHAPTER 3

Caples, John. Advertisement. 1926. US School of Music.

US School of Commercial Music. Internet. February 23, 2012. www.usschoolofmusic.com.

Sandhusen, Richard, *Marketing*. Haupauge, NY: Barron's Educational System, 2000.

Weiner, Matthew (executive producer), "Smoke Gets in Your Eyes," *Mad Men*, with performances by Jon Hamm. Lionsgate Television American Cable Network. AMC. July 19, 2007.

CHAPTER 4

Peterson, Erik, "No One Ever Got Fired for Buying IBM," *The Messaging Feed*, June 11, 2007, http://blog.corporatevisions.com/2007/06/11/no-one-ever-got-fired-for-buying-ibm/.

CHAPTER 5

Gray, John, *Men Are From Mars, Women Are From Venus: Practical Guide For Improving Communications And Getting What You Want In Your Relationships*. New York: Harper Collins, 1993.
Stone, Oliver (director). *Wall Street*, with performances by Charlie Sheen, Michael Douglas, and Tamara Tunie. Twentieth Century Fox Film Corporation, 1987.

CHAPTER 6

Fincher, David (director), *The Social Network*, with performances by Jesse Eisenberg, Andrew Garfield, and Justin Timberlake. Columbia Pictures, 2010.
Kübler-Ross, Elisabeth, *On Death and Dying*, New York: Scribner, 1969.
Stewart, James B. "Waiting for Gravity to Hit LinkedIn," *NYTimes.com*, July 8, 2011. www.nytimes.com/2011/07/09/business/gauging-if-linkedin-signals-a-social-networking-bubble.html?_r=2&pagewanted=all.

CHAPTER 7

Boyd, E. B., "Apple Can't Keep Up with iPad Demand." *Fast Company*, April 21, 2012, www.fastcompany.com/1748901/apple-cant-keep-up-with-demand-for-the-ipad.
Foley, James (director), *Glengarry Glen Ross*, with performances by Al Pacino, Jack Lemmon, and Alec Baldwin. New Line Cinema, 1992.
Knowles, Graeme, "A Conceptual Model for the Application of Six Sigma Methodologies to Supply Chain Improvement," *International Journal of Logistics: Research and Applications* 8, no. 1 (March 2005): 51–65.
Lohr, Steve, "Apple and I.B.M. Aren't All That Different." *NYTimes.com*, November 6, 2010, www.nytimes.com/2010/11/07/business/07unboxed.html.
Martin, Scott, "More Companies Put iPad to Work," *USA Today.com*, March 1, 2011, www.usatoday.com/tech/products/2011-02-28-ipad-enterprise_N.htm.

Reiner, Rob (director), *This Is Spinal Tap*, with performances by Rob Reiner, Michael McKean, and Christopher Guest. Embassy Pictures Corporation, 1984.

Zinnemann, Fred (director), *High Noon*, with performances by Gary Cooper, Grace Kelly, and Thomas Mitchell. Stanley Kramer Productions. 1952.

CHAPTER 9

Fernandez, Phil, "New Study Quantifies Dramatic Growth from Revenue Performance Management," *Modern B2B Blogs*, May 24, 2011, http: //blog.marketo.com/blog/2011/05/new-study-quantifies-dramatic -growth-from-revenue-performance-management.html.

Knowles, Graeme, "A Conceptual Model for the Application of Six Sigma Methodologies to Supply Chain Improvement," *International Journal of Logistics: Research and Applications* 8, no. 1 (March 2005): 51–65.

CHAPTER 10

Bishop, Matthew, "Multinationimbles," *Economist.com*, November 22, 2012, www.economist.com/node/17492958.

Crandell, Christine, "Customers Don't Read the Yellow Pages Anymore." *Forbes*. May 29, 2011.http://www.forbes.com/sites/christinecrandell /2011/05/29/customers-dont-read-the-yellow-pages-anymore/

"Fueling Business Growth Number One Issue for CEOs," The Conference Board. April 12, 2011, www.conference-board.org/press/pressdetail .cfm?pressid=4167.

Search, "Self-Help Book," www.amazon.com/s/ref=nb_sb_ss_sc_0_10?url =search-alias%3Daps&field-keywords=self-help+books&sprefix=self -+help%2Caps%2C300.

CHAPTER 11

"Michael Porter Value Chain Model Framework." ValueBasedManagement. net. Dec. 29, 2011. http://www.valuebasedmanagement.net/methods_ porter_value_chain.html

Antony, Jiju, "Pros and Cons of Six Sigma: An Academic Perspective," Improvement and Innovation.com. January 7, 2008, http://www.improve mentandinnovation.com/features/article/pros-and-cons-six-sigma -academic-perspective/.

Knowles, Graeme, "A Conceptual Model for the Application of Six Sigma Methodologies to Supply Chain Improvement," *International Journal of Logistics: Research and Applications* 8, no. 1 (March 2005): 51–65.

Stoermer, Nicole, "Lean Six Sigma Information," www.ehow.com/about
_6616247_lean-six-sigma-information.html.

CHAPTER 14

"Memorable Quotes from Lost In Space," 1998. Retrieved January 23, 2012,
http://www.imdb.com/title/tt0120738/quotes.

CHAPTER 15

Stoermer, Nicole, "Lean Six Sigma Information," www.ehow.com/about
_6616247_lean-six-sigma-information.html.

CHAPTER 16

Copeland, Chris. "From Intent to In-store: Search's Role in the New Retail
Shopper Profile." GroupM Research. October, 2011. http://www.scribd
.com/doc/68628887/From-Intent-to-In-store-Search-s-Role-In-The
-New-Retail-Shopper-Profile
Foley, James (director), *Glengarry Glen Ross*, with performances by Al Pacino,
Jack Lemmon, and Alec Baldwin. New Line Cinema, 1992.
"Inbound Marketing Methodology." The Inbound Marketing Company.
Retrieved: March 6, 2012. http://theinboundmarketingcompany.com
/inbound-marketing/inbound-marketing-methodology/
Jansen, Jim, "Online Product Research," *Pewinternet.org*, September 29,
2010, http://pewinternet.org/Reports/2010/Online-Product-Research
/Findings.aspx.
Schonfeld, Erick, "Share This Study: Facebook Accounts For 38 Percent
of Sharing Traffic On The Web," TechCrunch, June 6, 2011, http:
//techcrunch.com/2011/06/06/sharethis-facebook-38-percent-traffic/.
Scott, David M., *The New Rules of Marketing and PR: How to Use Blogs, Podcasting,
Viral Marketing & Online Media to Reach Buyers Directly*. Hoboken,
NJ: John Wiley & Sons, 2007.
Singer, Dirk, "The Top Three Spots on Google Get 58% of Clicks," *Lies Damned
Lies Statistics*, April 4, 2011, http://liesdamnedliesstatistics.com/2011/04
/the-top-three-spots-on-google-get-58-of-clicks.html.
Sterling, Greg, "Search + Social Media Increases CTR by 94 Percent:
Report," February 28, 2011, http://searchengineland.com/search-social
-media-increases-ctr-by-94-percent-report-66231.

"Successful Search Engine Positioning." *Get On Search Engine*. Retrieved March 6, 2012. http://www.getonsearchengines.com/ms-search-engine -positioning-ranking.php.

CHAPTER 17

"Business Technology Marketing Benchmark Guide Excerpt," Marketing Sherpa. 2007. http://www.marketingsherpa.com/exs/BusTech07Excerpt.pdf

Gschwandtner, Gerhard. "How Much Time Do Your Salespeople Spend Selling?" SellingPower Blog. Feb. 23, 2011. http://blog.sellingpower.com /gg/2011/02/how-much-time-do-your-salespeople-spend-selling.html

Miller, Jon, "The Definitive Guide to Sales Lead Qualification and Sales Development." Marketo Blogs. http://blog.marketo.com/blog/2011/03 /here-are-my-secret-methods-for-turning-marketing-leads-into -qualified-sales-leads.html.

Olson, Peggy Bekavac, "Leads, Leads, Leads—Part 3: Lead Nurturing," *The Green Sheet*, April 11, 2011, www.greensheet.com/emagazine.php ?story_id=2400.

CHAPTER 18

"94% of Leads Never Close? Ouch!" *Marketing Watchdog Journal* 63 (May 2009), http://mwj.bulldogsolutions.com/content/article052009_sirius.

Bash, Dana, "Cheney Accidentally Shoots Fellow Hunter," *CNN.com*, February 13, 2006, http://articles.cnn.com/2006-02-12/politics/cheney _1_katharine-armstrong-birdshot-saturday-afternoon-armstrong-ranch? _s=PM:POLITICS.

Conlon, Ginger. Reporter's Notebook: Sales Effectiveness Boosts Bottom-Line Results. *1to1Media*. February 2, 2009. http://www.1to1media.com /view.aspx?DocID=31357

Fernandez, Phil. *Cracking the RPM Code: A Look at Our Customers' Growth*. Marketo Blogs. http://blog.marketo.com/blog/2012/02/cracking-the -rpm-code-a-look-at-our-customers%E2%80%99-growth.html

Slayton, Doyle. "Cold Calling Dead Or Alive," *DiversifiedSolutions*, May 31, 2009, http://blog.diversifiedsourcingsolutions.com/2009/06/cold -calling-dead-or-alive.html.

CHAPTER 19

Brynjolfsson, Erik, "Strength in Numbers: How Does Data-Driven Decisionmaking Affect Firm Performance?" Cambridge, MA: MIT

Sloan School of Management, April 22, 2012, http://papers.ssrn.com /sol3/papers.cfm?abstract_id=1819486.

"John Wanamaker," *The Quotations Page*, January 23, 2012, www.quotation spage.com/quote/1992.html.

C<small>HAPTER</small> 20

Armstrong, Lance, *It's Not About the Bike: My Journey Back to Life*. New York: Penguin Putnam, 2000.

Asher, William (director). "Job Switching," *I Love Lucy*, with performances by Lucille Ball. CBS Television, Season 2, September 15, 1952.

"Bill Gates Quotes," Master of Business. January 23, 2012, www.billgatesmi crosoft.com/.

Bullen, Halsey, and Kimberley Crook, "Why We Need a Conceptual Framework," *FASB.org*, May 2005, www.fasb.org/cs/BlobServer?blobcol =urldata&blobtable=MungoBlobs&blobkey=id&blobwhere=117581882 5710&blobheader=application%2Fpdf.

C<small>HAPTER</small> 21

"Marshall McLuhan," *Searchquotes.com*, January 23, 2012, www.searchquotes .com/quotation/Advertising_is_the_greatest_art_form_of_the _twentieth_century./218165/.

Zhivago, Kristin, "Yes, Cats (Marketers) And Dogs (Salespeople) Can Actually Get Along And Work Together To Increase Your Sales," *Revenue Journal*, September 29, 2006, www.revenuejournal.com/2006/09/yes_cats_mar keters_and_dogs_sa_1.php.

C<small>HAPTER</small> 22

Ben-Zedeff, Sagee, "Telepresence Prepares the Ground for the Revolution. *RadVision Blogs*, August 30, 2010, http://blog.radvision.com/videooverenter prise/2010/08/31/telepresence-prepares-the-ground-for-the-revolution/.

"Che Guevara." *Quotations Page"* January 23, 2012. http://www.quotations page.com/quote/39723.html

Collins, Jim, *Good to Great*. New York: Harper Collins, 2001.

Knowles, Graeme, "A Conceptual Model for the Application of Six Sigma Methodologies to Supply Chain Improvement," *International Journal of Logistics: Research and Applications* 8, no. 1 (March 2005): 51–65.

"Napoleon Bonaparte." *Quotations.net*, January 23, 2012, www.quotations.net
/author-quotes/1644/Napoleon%20Bonaparte.

CHAPTER 23

Hayes-Finch, Mary. "Getting More Done with Less: How Lean Six Sigma
Enhances Performance." Goliath: Business Knowledge On Demand.
June 10, 2001. Retrieved March 7 2012. http://goliath.ecnext.com
/coms2/gi_0199-13006804/Getting-more-done-with-less.html.
Frigstad, David, "2008 Chairman's Series on Growth," Frost & Sullivan.
December 2, 2008, www.frost.com/prod/servlet/ebroadcast.pag?eventid
=126380616.
"Unknown." Quotes.net. STANDS4 LLC, 2012. 7 March. 2012. http://www
.quotes.net/quote/18392

CHAPTER 26

Fernandez, Phil, "New Study Quantifies Dramatic Growth From Revenue
Performance Management," *Modern B2B Blogs*, May 24, 2011, http://blog
.marketo.com/blog/2011/05/new-study-quantifies-dramatic-growth
-from-revenue-performance-management.html.
Weiner, Matthew (executive producer), "Smoke Gets in Your Eyes," *Mad Men*,
with performances by Jon Hamm. Lionsgate Television American Cable
Network. AMC. July 19, 2007.

CHAPTER 27

Foust, Dean, "Fred Smith on the Birth of FedEx," *BusinessWeek*, September
20, 2004, www.businessweek.com/magazine/content/04_38/b3900032
_mz072.htm.
Ross, Nikki, "Nice to Meet You. Would You Like to be friends or Friends?"
April 25, 2012, http://networkconference.netstudies.org/2011/04/nice
-to-meet-you-would-you-like-to-be-friends-or-friends/.
Slater, Robert. *Saving Big Blue: Leadership Lessons and Turnaround Tactics of
IBM's Lou Gerstner*. New York: McGraw Hill, 1999. Print.

INDEX

Accountability
  Chief Revenue Officer (CRO),
    201–203
  marketing, 31, 48, 76, 88–90, 101, 150,
    160, 171, 183, 201
  sales, 31, 48, 76, 84, 87, 88, 201
Agile Development, 67
Agility, 35, 37, 38, 61
Analytics, 20, 21. *See also* Revenue
  analytics
Appirio, 43
Apple iPad, 40–44
Armstrong, Lance, 170
Authenticity, 35–38
Automobile shopping process, 5, 6, 17
Aware stage of seed nurturing, 108, 109,
  116, 121, 122

"B2B Marketing and Sales Alignment
  Starts with the Customer"
  (Forrester Research), 75, 76
Bing, 118
Brand advocates, 3, 109
Brand awareness, 108, 109
Brand creation, 12
Brand names, 18, 21
Branding campaigns, 17
Business processes, 67, 69–71, 74, 82,
  100, 127, 160, 161, 163, 166, 168,
  170, 178, 198, 207
Business-to-business (B2B) transactions,
  17, 21, 75, 76, 85, 86
Business-to-consumer (B2C)
  transactions, 17
Buyers
  being found by, 98, 115
  considered (informed) purchases, 17,
    18, 21, 35

control of buying process, 3–6, 8, 9,
  15, 16, 26, 43, 78, 177
interaction with marketing during
  sales process, 25, 26, 31
interruptions and variations in buying
  behavior (nonlinear journey), 81,
  82, 108, 113
likelihood of purchase, 98. *See also*
  Lead scoring
needs, 63, 64
power shift from sellers to buyers, 34,
  35, 38, 39, 206
prospective buyers, inventory of, 98,
  155, 156, 160
research by, 78, 82, 116
technology and changes in sales
  process, 42, 43
Buying cycle, 25, 26, 54, 80–81, 104, 105,
  116, 127, 128, 134, 153
Buying signals, 129, 147

Carville, James, 3
Change
  commitment to, 65, 95, 206, 208
  impact of, 188
  marketing and sales dynamic, 62–64
  motivation for, 59, 60
  need for, 51, 55
  and opportunity, 59, 62
  revolutionary, 177–180, 209, 210
  sales and technology, 40–44
  value of, 60, 61
Cheney, Dick, 139
Chief Revenue Officer (CRO),
  198–203
Citrix Systems, 30, 191–197
Clinton, Bill, 3, 6
Cloud computing, 52, 96, 169, 191

marketing as investment in growth,
83–91
survey on marketing and sales
practices, 45–49
Revenue lifecycle, 147, 148
Revenue Performance Management
(RPM)
automation, 163, 164
change, revolutionary, 177–180,
209, 210
continuous measurement and
tracking, 70
demand chain reengineering, 51, 55
executive leadership, 185, 186, 189
forecasting revenue, 157–160,
178, 183
impact of, 51, 52, 54, 55
implementation, 95, 96, 181–189
and marketing and sales as art versus
science, 68, 69
Marketing Automation (MA) systems,
164–166, 170
metrics, 69–71, 160
playbook for, 191–196
and process transformation, 67
revenue cycle, 73–82
Revenue Cycle Model. *See* Revenue
Cycle Model
and revenue growth, 183
roadmap for, 205–208
and Six Sigma, 69–71
Software as a Service (SaaS), 169
software platform, 166–170, 186, 187
technology, 161–170
tools, 153
Zuora, 52–54
Revenue process, 9
Rosenberg, Craig, 27, 28

Sales
accountability, 31, 48, 76, 84, 87,
88, 201
as art, 68, 69, 74, 99, 172–174
change and technology, 40–44
closing, 39, 40
collaboration with marketing, 8, 9,
24, 25
compensation, 89, 90

continuous improvement, 74. *See also*
Continuous improvement
and customer interaction with
marketing, 25, 26
dysfunctional relationship with
marketing, 4, 5, 8, 9, 11, 15, 16,
23–29, 31, 65, 124, 184, 193, 209,
210. *See also* Sales-marketing
relationship, transforming
as expensive resource, 107, 108, 113
focus on most likely buyers, 99
high-growth companies, survey on,
45–49
hunting metaphor, 7–9, 18, 21, 105,
139–141
interaction with prospective buyers,
timing for, 107, 108
joint meetings with marketing, 30, 32
lead scoring, 144. *See also* Lead scoring
old strategies, 7, 8
personality types, 26, 28, 29, 32, 63
pipeline, 73, 74, 144
prioritization, 141, 143–146
productivity, 139–141, 144–146,
148, 168
as profit center, 24, 29
and revenue cycle, 78
social networks, use of, 8. *See also*
Social media
Sales cycle, 73, 74, 78, 80–82
Sales Development Representatives
(SDRs), 142, 143, 148
Sales force automation (SFA), 19
Sales funnel, 80–82, 112
Sales-marketing relationship,
transforming
initial steps, 30, 32
personal relationships, 31, 32
and revenue growth, 62–64
Sandhusen, Richard L., 13
Scott, David Meerman, 117
Search engine marketing (SEM),
118–120, 124
Search engine optimization (SEO),
116, 119
Seed nurturing phase (early awareness
and preference building)
about, 105, 113, 115–117